W9-BBH-097

Tea

DATE DUE			
10-29-85			

Teaching and Learning Languages

Earl W. Stevick

Cambridge University Press
Cambridge
London   New York   New Rochelle
Melbourne   Sydney

Published by the Press Syndicate of the University of Cambridge
The Pitt Building, Trumpington Street, Cambridge CB2 1RP
32 East 57th Street, New York, NY 10022, USA
296 Beaconsfield Parade, Middle Park, Melbourne, 3206 Australia

First published 1982
Reprinted 1983, 1983
Printed in the United States of America

Library of Congress Cataloging in Publication Data
Stevick, Earl W.
Teaching and learning languages.
1. Language and languages – Study and teaching. 1. Title.
P51.S854   407   81-18161
ISBN 0 521 24818 3 hard covers   AA CR2
ISBN 0 521 28201 2 paperback

British Library Cataloguing in Publication Data
Stevick, Earl W.
Teaching and learning languages.
1. Language and languages – Study and teaching
1. Title
407   P51
ISBN 0 521 24818 3 hard covers
ISBN 0 521 28201 2 paperback

Contents

Acknowledgements

Catherine Walter as reader for Cambridge University Press saw what I was trying to do and sometimes showed me ways in which I might do it better. I thank her for giving encouragement as well as criticism.

Others who have made helpful comments on drafts of the manuscript are: Victoria Badalamenti, a student in the MAT program of the School for International Training, Brattleboro, Vermont, USA; John Dumicich, Coordinator of In-Service Training, American Language Institute, New York University; Alice Hafn, of Brevskolan in Stockholm, Sweden; Peija Ilpola, of the University of Oulu, Finland; Becky Johnson, prospective teacher at the Language Institute of Japan; Jack Millet, of the staff of the MAT program in Brattleboro, Vermont, USA; Peter O'Connell, Principal, School of English Studies, Folkestone, England. To all these readers I am grateful for time and patience and insights. Responsibility for errors or inadequacies remains of course with me.

The School of Language Studies of the Foreign Service Institute has for twenty years been my professional home, and a continuing source of contact with the day-to-day realities of teaching and learning foreign languages.

Preface

A book is one person telling something to another whom he or she has never seen. Let me begin therefore by saying who I am and who I'm writing for. Since 1948, I've worked full time in one way or another teaching languages – first in English classrooms, then in training and in supervising teachers, and writing and consulting on materials in numerous languages for speakers of English. I've been at least a temporary learner in over a dozen languages and have also had different kinds of exposure to others. All of the students with whom I've worked directly have been adults. Against this background – in some ways broad, in others narrow – I've looked to see which things have worked and which have not, and made some guesses about *why* some things work well but others don't. With this book, then, I put into your hands, in a few pages, my summary of what I've seen and what my guesses are. For reasons of convenience, most of the examples I give will be in English. Many of them originated, however, in the teaching or learning of other languages.

This started out to be a book for teachers who are just beginning, no matter what their language or the age and level of their students. It has become also, in my own mind at least, a book for experienced teachers who are ready to take a fresh look at some of the things they've been doing all along, and to relate these things to how memory works and how people work together. Since I myself have never taught some types of class, this book lays no claim to being comprehensive. It concentrates on speaking skills, but even for oral classes it's an introduction, a sampler, not an encyclopaedia.

I hope this is a practical book, yet I don't want it to be a 'how-to-do-it' book. That is to say, I'm not going to give you one particular method – one matched set of techniques – and recommend that you follow it. There are already excellent methods books that do that, a few of which I mention in chapter 21. I cannot tell you what to read, partly because I cannot know which methods and which books you will be asked to use in the school or schools where you teach; partly also because I cannot know your personal preferences; most of all because I believe that whatever you do, you will do it better if you do it out of your own informed choices.

That is why this is not a 'how-to-do-it' book. Instead, I've tried to write a 'how-it-works' book. I've described a large number of techniques drawn from a wide range of methods – some old, some new, some widely used, some relatively unknown. It's only fair to warn you that you'll find highly competent experts in the field of language teaching who will tell you that certain of the techniques I've included here are outworn or at least outmoded. At the opposite extreme, other experts may call some of the techniques experimental or visionary. I hope, when they tell you this, that you will listen respectfully and learn from them. I can only assure you that the techniques I tell you about are ones that have worked in the past and will work again for teachers who see when, how and why they fit their students' needs. I've tried to make this an easy book to read, but one which will stay with you through much hard thinking.

PART 1　BEFORE YOU BEGIN

1　Between the people in the classroom

1.1　Introduction

> Good morning, class!
> Welcome to English 3!
> I'm ....
> First, I'll call the roll.

Here's a scene that repeats itself many hundreds of times a year in countries all over the world. This time though, it's different! *You* are the teacher! The course may be French 2, or Spanish 1, or Practical Portuguese, or Advanced Arabic instead of English 3, but the messages of these four lines are still there.

If you are reading this book, you probably haven't welcomed classes on many opening days. You may never have taught a language at all. In the following pages, I will pull together some of the things I have learned in 35 years, and set them out as clearly as I can for new language teachers. I hope you will find them useful. I also hope you will find them encouraging. Helping people to learn a new language is work, but it can be one of the most rewarding kinds of work there is. And it can be great fun!

The second part of this book will show you that you need never run out of classroom techniques. It will begin to answer your questions about 'How?' The third part will get you started on what you need to know concerning the workings of language – some of your questions about 'What?' The final chapter will steer you to a number of other books that will be of value to you as a new teacher. In this first part, though, let's take a few pages to look at the 'Who?' and the 'Where?' and the 'Why?' Unless you're fairly clear about these matters, your best techniques will be mere virtuosity, and your knowledge of linguistics may prove just so much excess baggage.

The words in the four sentences at the head of this chapter are

3

simple, and the sentences themselves make up a very common formula. Let's start by taking the formula apart. The assumptions that lie behind it are the framework within which you will probably be doing most of your teaching.

1.2 'Good morning, class!'

When you end the first sentence with the word 'class,' for example, you are recognizing your students as a very special kind of group. It is a group that has its meaning within a public school system, or a refugee program, or a university, or a commercial language school, or some other social institution. The members of the class, and the institution that they belong to, have their own goals for the course. Sometimes their principal goal is recreation or personal improvement. Sometimes it is simply the amassing of academic credits. Very often it is preparation for an external examination, or for a very specific type of employment. Some people have none of these 'instrumental' goals, but instead would merely like to identify themselves more closely with the culture that speaks German or Japanese or whatever the language is. This is what some people call 'integrative' motivation. But instrumental or integrative, the goal is never just 'to learn the language.' If this is true, then your own goal cannot be simply 'to teach the language.' Teaching a language is always a means toward other ends. When you called the people there in front of you 'class,' you accepted for yourself the role known as 'teacher,' and along with it an obligation to help your students to move toward the goals that they brought with them. This task may be made complex if the students' own goals are at variance with those of the institutions to which you and they are responsible, or if they differ among themselves as to goals, or if their goals are unrealistic. Complexity – even impossibility – does not detract from the priority of this task, however. Upon your success in dealing with it may depend much of your credibility, your acceptability and your professional existence.

Step 1. Find out what your students and their sponsors expect from the course.

1.3 'Welcome to English 3!'

When you 'welcome' your students to English 3, you are using the same word that you say to a guest who has come to your home. Using this word means first of all that you are speaking for the family that lives there. More important, though, it means that you intend to help your guest to feel comfortable. So we often follow 'Welcome!' with 'Make yourself at home!'

By watching a guest, we can get a pretty good idea of how well we have succeeded in making him[1] feel at home. Does he lean back on the sofa, or does he sit cautiously upright on the edge of it? Does he nibble politely just the minimum of food that custom requires him to eat, or does he eat heartily? Does he stay on the outskirts of the conversation, or does he seem to enjoy putting himself into it? Does he glance frequently at his watch, or does he seem to have lost track of the time?

The word 'welcome,' then, stands for one of the two essential sides to your role as teacher. You hope that by the end of the course your students will feel more at home with your language than they do now. You hope they will prefer to concentrate on the work at hand rather than on the clock. Most of all, you hope that they will throw intellect and imagination into the lesson, and not just go through the motions with their voices and their pencils.

This last point is particularly important. In the long run, the quantity of your students' learning will depend on the quality of the attention that they give to it. The quality of their attention will depend, in turn, on the degree to which they are able and willing to throw themselves into what is going on. And they will throw themselves in only to the extent that they feel secure in doing so. In this respect they're something like a turtle, which moves ahead on its own power only when it's willing to stick its neck out a little.

We all know that it's *nice* to make one's guests feel comfortable. But when you make your student-guests feel welcome and safe, you have done much more than just be nice to them. You have achieved a very practical end in opening the way for them

---

[1] The exclusive use of he, his, him in contexts like this perpetuates a tradition which is no longer acceptable. To use he or she (or she or he) and the corresponding double pronouns for possessive and objective forms is prohibitively awkward. No solution is likely to please everyone. My practice in this book will be to use the masculine forms in some chapters, feminine ones in others, and to envy the Turks, Japanese, and speakers of all other languages in which this issue does not arise.

to participate more freely in the course and to profit more fully from it.

We'll come back to this SECURITY → ASSERTION → ATTENTION formula when we look at what lies behind the fourth line of your opening words to your students. Meantime here's my next recommendation to you: *Step 2. Find out what will make your students feel welcome in your class and secure with you.* This will vary from one culture to another. For example, a very strict and heavy-handed style may frighten or offend students in one country, while in another country students may feel that a teacher who does not behave in that way is not a real teacher. Other examples come from body language: the way you use your eyes, the distance you stand from your students, the way you touch or refrain from touching them – all of these carry signals which will have a profound effect on your students' feelings of welcome and comfort with you. Such features of non-verbal communication are often subtle – so subtle that neither you nor your students are consciously aware of them. But aware or not, your students will be affected by them. In fact, the things we do that people don't consciously notice are often the very things that mold most deeply and firmly their attitudes toward us.

If you and your students are from different cultures, you may have quite a bit to learn about how they see teaching styles and nonverbal communication. Even if you and they share the same home culture, however, what I've just said still applies. Within any culture there is a vast range of effectiveness from one teacher to another, and much of the difference rests on just such matters as these.

This is not to say that your students' culture and the culture that you are representing to them are totally unlike each other, of course. Nor does it mean that all members of a particular culture are exactly the same in what makes them feel comfortable or uncomfortable. It goes without saying that you'll want to be sensitive to individual differences, but you're likely to misinterpret individuals unless you have a reasonably good picture of the culture out of which the individuals have come. So I repeat: your second step is to find out what means what in the culture(s) of your students. This will be a never-ending journey, of course. You certainly won't be able to complete it during your first few months as their teacher. You can make a significant start on it though, and that's what will be most important to you and to them.

All of this is part of treating your students as human beings with human needs. But they're not the only human beings in the classroom. You're one too, so it will be worth your while to notice what it is that makes you feel welcome or unwelcome, what would make you feel more secure so that you can put yourself more fully into your work with the class. Depending on your students' culture and your own, you may find it helpful to tell your students a bit about yourself, how you came to be their teacher, why you are doing things as you are, and so on.

There's another point to be made in connection with the second sentence of your opening monolog. In that sentence you are not merely making your students feel 'at home.' You are welcoming them to a very definite activity known as *English 3*. By enrolling in this course, your students are making a public commitment of themselves: of their time and money, most obviously, but also of mental effort and emotional resources. They want to feel that they are investing their minds and their emotions, their time and money, in a way that will bring them a satisfying return.

If you have followed steps 1 and 2, you have begun to find out what your students want, and something of what it takes to make them feel personally comfortable. But if they are seldom sure what kind of activity is coming next, they will have to divert a large part of their energy to figuring out what to try to do and when to try to do it. (Remember how much more tired you are after the first day on a new job than you are after you have learned the ropes and know what to expect.) Worse yet, if they sense that you the teacher aren't clear about what to do next, most groups will become uneasy and even demoralized.

Step 3, therefore: *Work out some basic techniques, and establish a simple, clear routine for using them.* You don't have to be inflexible either in the routine or in the techniques themselves. The important thing, though, is to keep from improvising too much – from looking as though you are making up your method as you go along. When the students sense that they are in firm hands, they can relax and turn their full attention to the task before them. If 'control' means establishing the rules for an activity and providing options among which students may choose, then you can maintain complete control in your classroom even while you allow your students to exercise a great deal of initiative. Think of a jungle gym – lengths of steel pipe joined together at right angles to make a rigid three-dimensional space within which children can climb about as they wish. Igor Stravinsky once remarked, 'My freedom will be so much the greater and more meaningful the more narrowly I limit my field of action and . . . surround myself with obstacles . . . The more constraints one imposes, the more one frees one's self of the chains that shackle the spirit.'

Frequent and significant 'initiative' within clear and dependable 'control,' as I have used these two terms, builds further the sense of security that is basic to the best kind of learning. An added advantage is that you as teacher will also feel more competent and therefore more confident when you are working in a familiar routine with tools that you know how to handle. This competence and confidence will come across to your students, increasing their security still further. (For this reason, most of the second part of this book is devoted to the devising of techniques and the establishing of routines.) Once they feel this confidence, you may find it profitable to sound them out from time to time about their reactions and their suggestions.

1.4 'I'm ....'

When you begin your third sentence with 'I'm,' you will really be saying, 'I, the teacher, am ....' Though details may vary from culture to culture and from school to school, a teacher is usually a person who directs what students are to do, who exercises power over them, and who evaluates what they have done. So you will say, in effect, 'I, the person into whose hands you are putting yourself to dominate you and direct you and judge you, am ....'

Watching myself over the years, as well as a number of other beginning teachers, I have seen at least five ideas of what a teacher's most basic function is. I began, I suppose, with a picture of a teacher who leaves people knowing more than they had known before. I remember several sessions in the class taught by one person who seemed to think that her essential duty was to correct mistakes; whenever the lesson was going so well that there were no errors, she did whatever was necessary to produce errors! Another teacher I knew acted as though her most important duty was to answer her students' questions. Others are certain that, above all, they must get their students through the textbook by the end of the course. Some are less concerned with subject matter, questions and errors, and more concerned with helping their students to become more capable and independent in dealing with the language on their own. My purpose here is not to say that some of these views are right and others are wrong, or even that one is better than another. But you may want to run this list through your mind, add to it if you can, and think about yourself and other teachers you have known.

Next in your opening words to your class, you complete that heavily loaded third sentence by giving the students your name. You may want to stop here for a moment and go back and read that sentence quietly, but aloud, to yourself. Insert your own name, in the form that your class will use in speaking to you. Pause for a few seconds to let the sound of the sentence echo a time or two through your mind. Then ask yourself, 'What is the person like who goes by this name? What brought her (or him) into the classroom, and what does she (or he) hope to get out of it?'

Let's look at just a few of the fringe benefits that go along with being a teacher, aside from the salary. For one thing, there's a certain amount of *infallibility*. Within your classroom and within the subject matter that you were hired to teach, you are always right. Even if you aren't always right, you know so much more than your students that it's very nearly the same thing. How important will that be to you the next time you step into a classroom?

Another fringe benefit is *power*: the right to tell people what to do and then tell them how well or how poorly they have done it. In this sense you will be standing in the shoes of your parents and your own teachers – of figures, that is, toward whom you felt love or fear or respect or perhaps some combination of emotions. As a teacher, you will feel that these emotions are being directed toward you. What does this status mean to you? How will you feel if people don't give it to you?

A third benefit that we teachers occasionally receive is *gratitude*. Are you able to enjoy your students' successes without demanding that they act grateful toward you?

Some artists use wood as their medium. Others use paint or musical instruments or dance. The medium for your creativity as a teacher will be the minds of other human beings. Books and curricula and visual aids are often called 'media,' but they are not the medium; they are only tools for working that medium. How do you feel about the pleasures, the responsibilities and the frustrations of working with other people's minds?

Would your prefer a strong sense of creativity accompanied

by little evident gratitude from your students, or enthusiastic gratitude for what you felt was a routine job of teaching? Similarly, how would you balance power against gratitude, power against creativity, or creativity against infallibility? These are some of the questions that may help you to understand better your own completion of the third sentence in your opening words to your class.

Step 4, then, is to *ask yourself these questions,* perhaps making a few notes. Then put those thoughts and those notes aside for a few days. Notice what additional answers come to you, perhaps when you least expect them.

1.5   'First, I'll call the roll.'

With the fourth and last sentence, you begin to read the students' names aloud one at a time. Have you ever noticed what people do when they first see a group photo which includes them? Each looks first, of course, to check on how he came out, and you can often overhear wry, self-conscious remarks on that subject. People react in very much the same way to a hand-lettered list that includes their names. And many (though not all) of us find it hard to let a mispronunciation of our names go uncorrected.

One obvious step that you can take, then, if you don't already speak your students' native language(s), is to learn to pronounce as well as possible these foreign names that belong to your students. More generally though, and much more important: *Step 5* is to take your first opportunity to *look at your students one at a time* – not while they're watching, of course. Spend about five seconds on each one. Remind yourself as you do so that here is one more ego laying itself on the line by becoming your student. Where you as teacher exercise your right and your responsibility to control what goes on in class, here is someone who is constantly being controlled. Where you are infallible, here is someone who expects to be evaluated every time he opens his mouth. The areas of your special knowledge are for him areas of ignorance. You may use your creativity in helping him to be creative also, but many teachers draw their feeling of creativity from their success in using their students' conformity to elicit lots of right answers. When your students feel that you are the *captive* of your own needs to display superior knowledge or to display superior power or to feel infallibility, gratitude or creativity, they may 'draw their heads back into their shells.'

But it's not just their relationship with the teacher that influences how students do in their studies. When a student feels in direct competition with other students, that feeling will affect performance, sometimes for the better and sometimes for the worse. Another strong force between students is loyalty, and pressure to conform to the standards of the class, or of the student's home culture. Too good an accent in speaking may be taken as a sign of willingness to move psychologically away from the life into which they were born, and toward becoming too much like the people whose native language the student is learning. Being too quick in any aspect of the course may set up tensions between a good student and his classmates. In even a small class the learning styles of the students may be dramatically different from one another; this too may lead to misunderstanding and impatience.

1.6 Conclusion

The five steps that I have suggested in this opening chapter will not of themselves make you into a good teacher. Moreover, many thousands of people through the ages have become good teachers without consciously following these steps. The most you can hope for, if you do follow them, is that they will bring you to a position from which you can see a bit more clearly where you are working and what you are working with.

2   Performance from three kinds of competence

2.1   Introduction

In 1957 I wrote a book titled *Helping people learn English.* While I was working on the manuscript, I didn't think very carefully about what I meant by 'learn.' To have 'learned' a language meant, obviously, to be able to understand it and produce it. I suspect that many of my colleagues in those days were for all practical purposes working from a definition about that simple.

In recent years, though, we've begun to see that there is more than one kind of 'learning,' just as there are several ways in which a person may 'understand' or 'produce' a given sentence. The differences aren't just theoretical, either. On the contrary, if you are aware of them, you will be able to see much more clearly what you and your students are doing in your work together.

2.2   'Performance' and 'competence'

In this chapter I will be talking about a set of distinctions that you may find helpful. Of these the broadest and simplest is between 'performance' and 'competence.'

> *Problem 1*
> You say: 'How long have you been studying English?' and your student replies: 'I have begun to study English two years ago.' What do you do?

In this exchange, your student's act of speaking is an example of performance. To have written the same sentence would also have been an act of performance, but in a different medium. In either case, her performance did not fit exactly with what natives would have said or written. We say that it 'was wrong,' or that it 'contained an error.' Her purpose in coming to your class in the first place was that she hoped you would help her to avoid just such errors. You, in turn, feel that errors in her performance show where you have not yet completed your mission as her teacher. So you set about getting correct performance from her. If you succeed, then both you and she will feel that your time has been well spent. The crucial question, though, is, 'Where will that correct performance come from?' The answer will depend very largely on what you did in order to elicit it.

You may, for example, come back with, 'I *began* to study English two years ago,' and signal the student to repeat the sentence after you. This is the fastest way to get the desired performance, but it is also the most superficial. As one of my students once remarked about corrections of that type, 'They go in your ear and out your mouth without disturbing anything in between.' They require very little – and so they tell you very little – about what the student has inside her that she will draw on the *next* time she speaks. These inner resources of the student are what linguists mean by competence. We can't observe competence directly. We can only make guesses about it on the basis of samples of performance. In one sense, all that the outside world cares about is performance because that is all that it can hear or see. Our most important task as teachers, however, is to help the student to build up the competence from which her future performance must flow. Unless, of course, we expect to be at her elbow for the rest of her life whispering each correct sentence as she needs it! Or unless we are coaching her for a very specific examination!

When you have the student simply repeat the correct sentence after you, therefore, you are demanding of her only the most rudimentary kind of competence: she must be able to hear you and to repeat what you have just said. She may also notice where the model that you have set for her differs from what she said in the first place, but even that is not necessary. This much competence is more than nothing. After all, a complete beginner will be unable to repeat sentences as long as the one in my example. For other students, however, the kind of correction in my first example does nothing to stretch the student's competence; it therefore contributes little toward making that competence grow.

The same is true for a correction which you give by writing a word or by pointing to a word that has already been written. You are again demanding a very shallow kind of competence. When your student comes up with the right performance on the basis of some bit of competence, the experience of having succeeded will strengthen that competence. In itself, however, this experience of success will not very much deepen or expand the competence. Deepening and expansion of competence will come only if the student has – and takes – time to think about what she has done and why.

In a third way of dealing with errors you force your student to do just that. You say, 'You . . .?' This is enough to tell the student that there is an error and to tell her that the error is located immediately after the last word you repeated, but she still has to provide the correct wording for herself. This kind of correction may (or may not) take more time than the first and second kinds. It may (or may not) break up the rhythm of class activity – or it may require you to shift to a slower, more subtle rhythm. The advantage, of course, is that the student's success now must come either from recall of something that she had not yet completely mastered, or from use of reasoning, or from both. In any event, what is strengthened by this kind of success will be something that is clearer, more detailed, and more useful than a mere general ability to repeat or to read a correct answer that has come from someone else.

In a fourth style of correction you merely indicate, perhaps by gesture or facial expression, that there is an error somewhere, but you don't specify where. This is very much like the third style except that it demands and develops an even broader and deeper kind of competence.

A fifth style of correction doesn't appear to be correction at all. You simply continue the conversation in the same tone of voice you would have used if the student had spoken correctly. You manage, however, to put in something which will be likely to get a correction from the student: 'You say you began to study English two years ago?' or 'You began *three* years ago?' or 'I'm sorry! *When* did you begin . . . ?' This kind of implicit correction requires that the student be alert to linguistic form even while she continues to be absorbed in what both of you are saying to each other. It is therefore trickier than the first four. But the skill which it demands, rewards and strengthens is one that will be invaluable to the student both in your class and after she has left you.

In describing these five kinds of correction, I don't mean to tell you that one of them is somehow better than another. I have only listed some of the options that are available to you. Each has its advantages and its disadvantages. You yourself, from day to day and from moment to moment, will have to balance speed, rhythm, depth and anxiety against one another and make your own choices.

The kind of competence that we have been talking about up to this point is obviously complex, and it exists on more than one level of abstraction. In order to produce the word *began* in the sentence 'I .... to study English two years ago,' for example, a person must know how to produce at least these two vowels and three consonants fairly well; must know the meaning associated with them; must know that the past form is *began* and not *beginned* or *begon* or something else – or must arrive at the correct form by analogy with some other verb such as *sing*; and must be aware that a time expression that ends with *ago* (and does not begin with *since*) rules out any present perfect form like *have begun*. You may be able to think of other prerequisites for this particular bit of performance.

All of the items that I listed in the preceding paragraph are examples of one kind of competence, called 'linguistic competence.' For many years this was the only kind of competence to which language teachers gave serious attention. It was limited pretty much to the relationships between individual words and meanings, and to the relationships among words and parts of words within single sentences. The performance to which this kind of competence led was the production of correct sentences.

2.3 Communicative competence

Problem 2

You (with your arms full of books): 'Do you think you could open that door?'

Student (without moving to open the door): 'Yes, I do.'

This student has not responded in the way you had hoped she would. She has apparently understood your sentence all right, and her reply is grammatically correct. She has said 'Yes, I do,' and not 'Yes, I think' or 'Yes, I think it' or something similar. Yet she has still failed to understand you in the way that any native speaker would. In the grammar of individual sentences, a question is 'a request for information,' and that is exactly how your student has treated it. Yet we all know that questions are in fact one of the most common ways of making a polite request. According to the grammar of individual sentences, the making of requests is a function of the imperative, and the word *please* makes a request polite. Yet I, at least, am unable to think of any tone of voice that would keep the sentence 'Open the door, please' from sounding like a command that is either peremptory or a little condescending.

In the same way all native speakers know that the imperative sentence 'Imagine that!' is not really a command or request, but an exclamation of amazement. 'I'm not sure what you want' is a request for information, and anyone who responds to it as though it were a mere statement of fact will be considered impolite. I think that all native speakers of English will agree with me in these judgments. Insofar as they do agree, then our agreement must be based on some sort of inner resources which we all share, which we use in speaking to and understanding one another. These resources are included in a kind of knowledge which is different from and broader than 'linguistic competence.' Theorists have begun to call it 'communicative competence.'

We don't yet know as much about communicative competence and how it is learned or taught as we know about linguistic competence. Nevertheless, there are a few points which you may want to keep in mind about these two goals of language study.

1. Inadequacies in linguistic competence show up in performance as rather clearly defined errors which are relatively easy to pick out and correct. Performance errors that result from faulty communicative competence sometimes stand out clearly, as in the examples I have already given. More often, however, they're hard to put your finger on.

2. Perhaps for that reason, a few linguistic errors are enough to camouflage the existence of a communicative problem. Hearing a foreign pronunciation or a wrong verb tense, we simply conclude, 'This person is a foreigner,' and so are not surprised if in addition to talking funny she also acts a little strange.

Here's an imaginary conversation between two university students, at least one of whom is a non-native speaker of English. How many linguistic errors can you find in it, and how many evidences of incomplete communicative competence? If you stop and make a list, I think you'll find that the former stand out much more clearly than the latter.

    — Hi! How are you today?
    — Thank you. How are you?

— OK, I guess. Hey! Aren't those new glasses you're wearing? They really look good on you!

— Don't be foolish. I buy them because I cannot find good ones. I look terrible in them!

— No, I really like them. By the way, have you registered yet?

— Yes, I am just finish.

— Did you sign up for any history courses this term?

— Oh yes. I like very much the history. I will take History 421.

— Really? I'm taking it too. So I'll be *seeing* you! Do you think . . .

— Good bye.

In this conversation there are at least three points at which the first speaker may have thought that the second speaker was acting a bit strange. First, he didn't say 'Fine!' in reply to 'How are you today?' Second, he seemed to be fishing for further compliments about his new glasses. Finally, he broke off the conversation while the first speaker was in the middle of a question to him.

In fact, each of these bits of 'strangeness' can be traced to a gap in the second speaker's communicative competence. He did not know that in English 'Fine!' (or some equivalent) is required in reply to 'How are you?' but 'Thank you' is optional. In his home culture, the reverse is true. He did not know that the most graceful thing to do with a compliment is to accept it briefly and then go on to talk about something else. Again, he was following what he had been taught at home. And although he knew that 'I'll be seeing you' sometimes functions as a leave-taking, he did not recognize that in this particular context it retained its literal meaning as a prediction. The details are not important here. My point is that manifestations of communicative (in)competence are usually subtle — so subtle that they lead to misinterpretations, the existence of which is recognized by neither party.

3. Linguistic competence can be strengthened through drills which consist of single sentences or parts of sentences:

	I began studying English two years ago.
last year	I began studying English last year.
in 1981	I began studying English in 1981.
as a child	I began studying English as a child.
	etc.

or:

I began studying English two years ago.	Oh! You've been studying it for two years?
I began studying English last year.	Oh! You've been studying it since last year?
I began studying English in 1981.	Oh! You've been studying it since 1981?
etc.	etc.

Communicative competence cannot come out of mechanical drills like these. It consists, after all, in knowing what to do with (grammatically correct) sentences in larger contexts. Communicative meaning depends on a much wider range of factors than linguistic meaning does. As you help your students to develop communicative competence, therefore, at least two things must happen: (1) You must provide them with samples of language in use – samples which are long enough to bring in the full range of factors, whether the length of a paragraph or a novel. (2) Your students must take part imaginatively in what is happening in the sample. You may also (3) discuss with your students the parts that various words and sentences play in the whole.

2.4 Personal competence

These, then, are two dimensions within which you will be of greater or less help to your students: developing their communicative competence (knowing what to say) and perfecting their linguistic competence (knowing how to say it). These two dimensions contain the goals laid down in course syllabi, and the objectives with which the writers of textbooks begin their work. There is, however, a third dimension without which these first two can lead at best to an academic, flat, sterile achievement. The question is whether as teacher – or how much, as teacher – you can hope to help your students in this third dimension. I'm not sure, but let me set before you, briefly, what I see here.

The third competence is personal. Like linguistic and like communicative competence, it exists on many levels of abstraction. I will list four.

On the most superficial level, a student needs to have at his command techniques – things he knows how to do – which he can use with new material. Given a list of words, for instance, some students simply panic. They are the ones who lack even a single way of dealing with this kind of challenge. As I am using the term, they are in this respect totally 'incompetent.'

Few, of course, remain totally incompetent for very long. Either by their own devising or through the example of their classmates or their teacher they at least discover flash cards. Now they are minimally competent in this third, this personal dimension. They will grow in this dimension by adding new techniques. Some simple ones are to say the words aloud many times to themselves, alone but in a voice that's firm and carries confidence; to make up in their own minds bizarre images connected to the words; to devise flash cards in which the second side contains not their native language, but some short phrase in which the foreign word would fill a blank; to write each word a dozen times; to pick a list of five or ten words and try to write them out from memory a few times in the target language. Students can learn not only the techniques themselves but also how to time them: how long to work on a set of flash cards at one sitting, for example, and how long to wait before going through them a second, third or fourth time.

On this first level, there is obviously much that you can do to add to your students' personal competence. You can even cast your contribution in the form of very concrete and explicit 'behavioral objectives': 'The students will be able to describe and exemplify at least three ways of working with new vocabulary lists' or the like.

This first level of personal competence provides raw materials for a second, but it does not of itself guarantee that much will happen on that second level. Beyond merely knowing a range of techniques for memorizing vocabulary or for mastering new grammatical patterns or for improving pronunciation, each student can become aware of just how her mind functions in a given technique, and of which techniques are most effective for her. Students differ greatly from one another in this respect. This second level of competence thus leads to an ability to make for oneself a series of independent choices about how to work.

On this second level, your contribution as teacher is not quite so easy to state in the form of a set of 'behavioral objectives.' Nevertheless, there are at least three things that you can do that will make growth on this level more likely. Most basic, you can enrich the first level, as long as you don't expose your students to so many options that they become confused. Second, you can make it clear (more through how you act than through what you say) that you do not think some of the alternative techniques are inherently more 'scientific,' more elegant, doctrinally sounder, *or more acceptable to powerful you* than others. Let the only criterion be effectiveness. Third, you can provide opportunities for your students to compare two or more techniques with one another and to talk very briefly with you or among themselves about their observations. If in this sort of exchange you can remain at the same time interested and nonjudgmental, you will do more than most of my language teachers ever did toward fostering the growth of personal competence.

On a third level, students may become aware of how they go about adopting a new technique or modifying an old one. What you contribute on the first level can be done almost mechanically, and what you contribute on the second can at least be scheduled. On this third, more abstract level, however, neither you nor your students can call forth examples at will. If you are to be of help here, you will have to recognize these insights first in yourself. Then you may be able, in something that a student says or does, to recognize that this further kind of growth is taking place. If you do see it, work with it. Comment briefly or not at all. Whatever you do, don't talk it to death! But know that something in your teaching may have been right.

So far, we've been talking about 'personal competence' in dealing with the cognitive side of language learning. We have ignored the emotions – strong or weak, positive or negative – that inevitably accompany the experience. But because emotions have such a profound effect on the success or failure of language study, they must be dealt with: someone must deal with them. Here is the fourth level in personal competence – the most subtle and the most stubborn level. If you see negative emotions interfering with your students' progress, you can change what you are doing and so set matters at least partly right. But you are only human, and you are dealing with a group of other humans who may be quite unlike each other. Therefore sometime, in some way, to some extent, each of them must answer for and to herself how she reacts to difficulty, frustration, humiliation, or what seems to be unfairness. Here again, each person needs more than one mode of reacting, needs to know how to choose among these modes, and needs to know how she learns or modifies new modes. With this fourth level we have passed beyond the bounds of language teaching in its narrow sense. I do not think, however, that we have passed beyond the bounds of education.

3 Learning, acquiring, remembering, and producing language

3.1 Learning and acquiring

There are a few questions which have occupied language teachers for centuries and probably always will. Of these perhaps the most basic is 'How does a person come to control a language anyway?' We all achieved this feat with our first language, and many of us have gained some ability in other languages by studying them in school. The term 'acquisition' is sometimes used for the former, and 'learning' for what goes on in the classroom. There has been considerable discussion about whether these two processes are essentially the same, or essentially different. Until very recently, however, people have generally assumed that one followed the other with perhaps a few years' overlap. The ability to 'acquire' supposedly died out at about the age of puberty, while 'learning' became possible only in the early school years as the necessary 'readinesses' developed.

More recently, though, some research has indicated that the picture is not quite like that. It may be that the same kind of acquisition we see in children can continue well into adulthood – perhaps throughout life. Or it may be that what some people call 'adult acquisition' is really a third process. Be that as it may, however, it is becoming clear that adults and adolescents do have available to them at least two modes of gaining control of a new language.

The better known of these two modes is (in a special, narrowed sense) called 'learning.' Here, learning begins with selection of some clearly defined element which is to be learned. In helping someone else to learn, your job is to teach (again in a specially restricted sense of that word). In teaching, you first present the new item as clearly and interestingly as you can. Then you have your students practice the item in one way or another until they seem to have got it. When the time comes, you go on to test them on it. Finally, you may or may not get around to using it with them in some communicative way.

In this kind of teaching and learning, then, the very act of selecting an item pulls it out of the context of normal communicative exchange. To compensate for this severing of the normal interrelationship you may go to some length to provide context as you present, drill and test it.

In acquisition, the person who is doing the acquiring meets words in the full context of some kind of genuine human communication. There is no special presentation of a new item, no organized drilling, and no testing in the academic sense. Conversation is about things which the acquirer understands and which are already clear in his mind. Because a teacher cannot read minds, this requirement commonly means that in the beginning most of the conversation will be about what is present in the classroom at the time. The language used is generally at a level which the acquirer already controls *or a little beyond that level*. The acquirer follows the discourse comfortably, drawing on context to fill in the meanings of new words and constructions. In time he becomes able to produce new items correctly, but for a while he may remain largely silent. When he does speak, those around him react in terms of their attempts to communicate, and not in terms of the correctness or incorrectness of what he has said.

This kind of acquisition takes time and patience. Until a student has acquired an item, he will make numerous errors in its use. Learning, by contrast, produces correct forms almost immediately.

There are however some weighty advantages to acquisition as compared with learning. What has been learned may be forgotten after (or before!) the next test, while what has been acquired is relatively permanent. What has been acquired serves directly as the basis for smooth production either of speech or of writing. Learned material is useful for monitoring, correcting or translating what has originated from material which has already been acquired either in the target language or in the native language, *but not for much else*. Not least, learning will work only for those items which can be stated fairly simply: English *house* corresponds to Spanish *casa*, for example, and the ending -*s* is used only for English verbs which are in the present tense with a third person singular subject. Acquisition works for everything: for all of the matters that I've just mentioned, but also for phonetic nuances, use of definite and indefinite articles, choice of just the right preposition or verb tense, and so on. The essential difference between learning and acquisition may lie in what the student does with what is put in front of him, but many parts of a language simply defy anyone to perform learning on them!

Over the centuries language teachers have used countless methods and techniques. Most of the time, by whatever method, we have concentrated on trying to teach so that our students would learn. Acquisition has come – when it has come at all – as a desirable but incidental by-product of good teaching and good learning. Its recent identification as a separate process casts light on what we have been doing all along. This knowledge also opens up exciting new prospects for what we may do in the future. Now that we see the difference between learning and acquisition, we can balance them against each other and combine them so that each will promote the other.

This, then, is a contrast which is worth exploring. Having said that, let's turn and look at one respect in which the two are special cases of a single phenomenon. That phenomenon is the storage and retrieval of memories.

3.2   Remembering and producing

In recent years there has been a great deal of fascinating research on human memory. One of the most basic facts which that research has brought to light is that what we think of as separate items are not stored separately. In talking with audiences about memory, I have many times asked people to call to mind some word which they have learned recently either in a foreign language or in their native language. Once they have identified such a word I ask them a series of questions: At what time of day did you learn it? Where were you? Which way were you facing? If you learned the word out of a book, where was it on the page? Was the type large, or small? If you learned the word from a person, where was that person? What general tone of voice did he or she use? What was the weather like? In general, people can come up with immediate and confident answers to questions such as these. *Sensory data that come together are stored together.*

Bringing back one item in an image also tends to bring back the other items in that same image. A well-known example of this principle is the power of odors to give vivid recollections of certain places or people: a whiff of coal smoke will always carry me back to Nashville in the mid-1950s, and lavender to the street corner in Yugoslavia where I once bought a vial of it. In the same way a couple may refer to a piece of music as 'our song' because it has the power to restore the sights and sensations of some time early in their courtship.

This does not mean that all items in a given image are equally clear and accessible, of course. We've all had the experience of remembering a face or a set of initials but not being able to come up with the name that goes with them. And going back to an earlier example, we know what it's like to see exactly where that grammatical rule was on the page, but not to be able to 'read' it. Nevertheless the other items in the image are there if only we could get at them. In chapters 4 and 5, we'll look in more detail at this sort of experience with memory.

A second basic fact about memory is related to this first one: *we can summon up two or more images, examine them, select items from each one, and form a new composite image that consists of parts of the old ones.* Again we find simple and well-known examples in our attempts to remember people's names: if I'm introduced to a man named O'Farrell, the name calls back an image which contains the name Farrell's – a chain of ice cream restaurants in the area where I live. I picture this man entering one of these establishments, being surprised, and exclaiming 'Oh!' Then I store the new image in the hope that the next time I see his face it will bring the rest of the image back in a way that will enable me to call Mr O'Farrell by his name.

A third observation about these images (and then we will be ready to go back and look at learning and acquisition again): *every image contains auditory elements (if only silence), visual elements (if only darkness), emotional elements (if only boredom or indifference), tactile elements, olfactory elements, and elements representing the state of the body at the time the image was formed.* In any one image the items in, for example, the visual dimension may be many or few. Moreover, the various elements in a single image may be very closely integrated with one another. That is to say, they may fit together in such a way that a change in one would require a corresponding change in others. Or they may be merely juxtaposed with only a minimum of integration.

Images that come from outside the foreign-language classroom are almost always well integrated. This is not necessarily the case inside the language classroom, however. Take the cliché sentence 'The book is on the table.' If you are leaving the room just as I enter it and you know that I've come for a certain book, and if you want to be helpful, you may say exactly that sentence to me. Then your speaking it will be part of an image in which motive, physical situation and language are well integrated with one another. But suppose you say that sentence only because I have just said, 'The pen is on the table. Book.' Perhaps there's no book within sight at the time, or perhaps there is. It doesn't make any difference. You are responding only to my words – to one tiny segment of your sensory intake at the moment. You are also responding to two very non-specific motivations of your own – your desires to practice a pattern and to please me.

If in the same classroom instead of 'The pen is on the table. Book.' I had said 'We are here. Negative.' and you had responded with 'We are not here,' the other elements in the total input image would have remained unchanged. This is an example of what I mean by an unintegrated image.

Sometimes we try to enrich an image and integrate it by using visual aids to illustrate what we have our students say: a book on the table one time, and a pen another time. This at least integrates a small part of the visual dimension with the linguistic dimension. But the motivational and social elements that would fit the words are still lacking. Even when we set up games in which students have to exchange or pool information which not all of them have, the motivational and social elements *may* still be of kinds which are seldom found outside the language classroom.

3.3 Conclusion

Now we are ready to take another look at learning and acquisition. It may be that both these processes are examples of what I have been saying about the storage, retrieval and reconstruction of images. The difference between them lies in the nature of the images. In acquisition the image from which we reconstruct what we are after is rich and well integrated, while in learning it is impoverished and unintegrated. The higher the quality of the image – that is, the richer and better integrated it is – the more easily we will be able to get back one part of it when we encounter another part. In addition, the affective side of what we acquire is usually of a kind which causes us to welcome the recall of an image. The affective side of some learning experiences is pleasant, but many of them contain heavy elements of feeling ignorant, powerless and constantly evaluated – the kinds of anxiety that I mentioned in chapter 1. When that is the case, a learned image may in some deep sense be unwelcome even at a time when our most obvious but more superficial motivations (the need to get a good grade or to sound educated, for example) make us try desperately to get it back.

If what I have said in the preceding paragraph is correct, then the modes of getting a new language which are available to a student are not exactly two in number. What we have been calling acquisition and learning now become only the ends of a continuum which rests on a single process. Both operate according to principles that are already familiar from research on memory. It seems to me that this conclusion throws light on both ends of that continuum without minimizing the differences between them and without diminishing the urgent need to tell them apart and to exploit both of them.

The characteristic product of learning, then, is *fragments*. One serious limitation of learning is that those fragments do not support one another in the learner's mind the way the pieces of a completed jigsaw puzzle do. Instead they lie in the learner's mind like unassembled pieces of the puzzle of real communication, neatly stacked in little piles according to color or size or other abstract criteria. So it is hardly surprising that what we have learned cannot serve us directly when we have something that we really want to say.

Wouldn't it be a good idea then to do away with learning altogether and concentrate our efforts on promoting acquisition? I don't think so. We've already seen that acquisition is a relatively slow process. In addition to that it may have its own characteristic product, which is not fragments but *fossils*. We all know people (perhaps we ourselves are such people!) who live for ten, twenty or more years in a foreign country conducting their daily affairs in the language of that country – who are, in other words, right in the middle of a genuine acquisition setting – but who persist in the same errors of pronunciation and grammar. Their competence in the language has 'fossilized' short of becoming identical with the competence of native speakers. If that can happen in life outside the classroom, how much sooner and how much more easily can it happen inside the classroom! Apparently people acquire as much of a language as they *really* need for what they *really* want, but only that much. One person really wants nothing to do with the foreign culture.

That person will 'acquire' little or nothing. Another just wants to do necessary shopping and exchange a few simple greetings. Another wants to transact all his business with the native speakers fluently. Another is attracted to the culture and desires to become as much like the native speakers as possible. Given the same opportunities, each of these people will acquire a different amount of the language, but only the last is likely to carry the process to completion. Your success in helping people to acquire language in a classroom will therefore depend not only on the techniques you use, but also on how you, and what you do, affect their attitudes toward the language and the people who use it.

Learning and acquisition, then, are separate strands which you as teacher will wind together so that they supplement each other. Just how much you use of each will depend on your students. With some classes you will be able to discuss this matter openly with your students and then either work according to their preferences or work to change their preferences. In any case, you won't be able to wind the strands into a strong cable until you have seen the difference between them, and until your fingers have found out how to bend them and direct them.

The need to balance 'acquisition' and 'learning' against each other is not new to language teachers. We used to get at some of the same issues when we talked about the relationship between 'accuracy' and 'fluency.' When I was being trained, back in 1949, there was a clear rule: 'accuracy before fluency.' We assumed that a student's mind was like a clay tablet into which lines were being carved, one with each utterance, so as to produce the grooves – the linguistic competence, as we called it in chapter 2 – which would guide future performance. Any error, and particularly any uncorrected error, would contribute toward the wrong kind of groove, and so should be avoided.

Another assumption which lay behind the 'accuracy before fluency' maxim was that 'fluency' is simply the result of a large amount of practice. The formula was really an abbreviation for 'sufficient practice of accurate forms leads to the desired kind of fluency.'

Nowadays, we realize that the picture is not so simple as we used to think. For one thing, 'competence' is not two-dimensional like the grooves in a clay tablet, and what a learner practices is the mobilization of competence (chapter 1), not just the repetition of performance. For another, fluency depends at least as much on emotional factors as on amount of practice, and too much insistence on accuracy can erode this essential foundation of fluency.

In summary, no-one (I hope!) suggests that either accuracy or fluency be abandoned in favor of the other. The question about maintaining accuracy is not 'whether'; it is 'when' – and 'how.'

4 One set of metaphors for memory

4.1 Introduction

I said earlier that our minds work with *images*: more or less rich
and more or less well integrated configurations of stimuli that
come in together through all of our senses. Let me now change
the emphasis in that sentence and say that our minds *work* with
those images. As a teacher you need to know some of the ways
in which different people's minds do that work. First, a few
points that seem to be true for just about everyone.

4.2 Short-term memory, long-term memory, permanent memory

One of the most important of these points is a difference
between short-term memory (STM), long-term memory (LTM)
and permanent memory (PM). Our short-term memory for what
we hear is in fact *very* short – perhaps only 20 or 30 seconds.
This is how long something that has just come in through the
ears will remain available without being repeated. Think of the
images that are in STM at any given moment as a group of
stencils lying on a fairly small worktable. As new stencils are
constantly added, older ones get pushed off the table onto the
floor and are lost. (By 'stencil' I of course mean the kind we use
for labeling cartons and crates – not the kind used in mimeo-
graphing.)

If any of these stencils – these images, these facts – are to be
available for more than half a minute, they must be put up on
the wall behind the worktable where the learner can find them
when she needs them. Imagine further that the only way the
learner can make these paper stencils adhere to the wall is to rub
them vigorously with a stick until they accumulate a charge of
static electricity. This charge will hold them on the wall for a

relatively long time. The duration of LTM as measured in experiments is a matter of hours or days. But just as the static charge on the paper stencils gradually dissipates, so the strength of LTM declines with the passage of time. Whether new material makes it from STM to LTM at all, and how long it remains there, are largely affected by how much work the learner's mind does on it while it is still on the STM worktable.

LTM, then, is like a very large wall displaying many paper stencils which are held in place by stronger or weaker static charges. All of these stencils will eventually fall to the floor, and with them the information that they contain. In order to keep that information indefinitely, the learner must spray them with paint while they are still on the wall. She may do so as soon as a stencil is affixed to the wall, or just before it falls to the floor, or at some time in between. The effect will be the same: the image will remain as long as the wall stands. This is what happens when material moves from LTM to PM. But the amount that gets transferred is generally much less than the complete original image – sometimes as little as a fragment of one word. We can seldom cover a whole stencil with one blast from the spray can.

The factors which contribute toward retention were traditionally grouped under the three headings 'recency,' 'frequency' and 'intensity' of exposure to what a learner wants to remember. Let's see how these three factors might have tied in with STM, LTM and PM.

Whether or not a particular image is still in STM depends mostly on recency – the 20–30 second figure that I cited earlier. Whether it makes it into LTM is pretty much a matter of frequency and intensity: how many times and how hard we rub the stencil. But getting from LTM into PM is, I suspect, dependent mostly on intensity.

One thing that you as a teacher should know about frequency is that there seems to be a very important difference between what the experimenters call 'massed practice' and 'distributed practice.' What this means is that if you give one learner ten exposures to some item but these exposures are interrupted by exposures to other items, she is more likely to retain that item than is another learner whose ten exposures to that item were all in one bunch.

The term 'intensity' covers a number of aspects of the learner's experiences. Most obviously it includes what might be termed the 'vividness' of exposure to an item: other things being equal, a color picture will be remembered longer than a black and white picture; a sentence spoken by a skilled actress will make more of an impression than the same sentence read in the 'now-listen-carefully' drone used by some teachers. 'Intensity' also includes the long-term importance of what is said: a person who expects to visit Canterbury soon will be more likely to retain material out of *Murder in the cathedral* than will a person who has no such expectation. Of particular interest to teachers, it includes in addition the emotional 'depth' at which the material touches the hearer, and the cognitive 'breadth' of the associations that the material finds in the hearer's mind. Depth and breadth are partly under your control as you lead your students in thinking and talking about the things they are learning, and even in responding to them with physical actions.

In summary, then, a new item needs only one intense experience in order to attain status in PM. (I am sure this is an oversimplification, but I don't think it is misleading.) Its chances of receiving the necessary intensity increase with the total number of exposures; the number of exposures can be greater the longer the image stays in LTM; the chances of transmitting a clear and full image to LTM are in turn increased by repeating the item several times and thus re-entering it into STM – putting it back on the tabletop where it can be worked on again and again. There has been a fair amount of research on getting things from STM into LTM, but much less on crossing from LTM to PM.

These stencils that I've been talking about are not made of steel, but of paper. That is to say, we can cut them into pieces and use our STM worktable in order to construct a new composite image which we may treat in just the way we treated the images that came in from outside. Such an internally-manufactured image may or may not make it into LTM and PM, depending on the same factors of recency, frequency, intensity, etc., that we have already discussed.

4.3 Images, patterns and rules

Let's move on now and look at the relationships among images and patterns and rules. By 'image' I mean the same more or less rich and well integrated memory configuration that we've been talking about. Such an image might include the items:

      wait   waited

But these items are in a language that you know very well. My next definition will be clearer if I also give you an example in a language that you may not know. The same kind of image might just as well include the items:

kiti   viti

In the next few paragraphs I'd like to use 'pattern' to mean 'whatever

wait   waited

and

load   loaded

have in common.' In the Swahili example we will look at a pattern represented by:

kiti   viti
kiberiti   viberiti

People recognize and use patterns like these even if they have never thought about them explicitly or heard them summarized in words. Indeed, small children could not otherwise come out with (incorrect) forms like:

*rided[1]
*standed

except by following the kind of pattern I have cited. You, too, in Swahili, can follow the pattern of the above examples, and from *kisu* you can produce the (correct) form *visu* even if I haven't told you that these pairs of words are singular and plural forms of nouns.

By 'rule' I mean any kind of explicit statement about a pattern: 'In English, if a regular verb ends with -*t* or -*d*, the past is formed by adding an extra syllable spelled -*ed*.' 'In Swahili, a noun whose singular has the prefix *ki*- forms the plural with the prefix *vi*-.'

If we may use these three terms for a moment as I have defined them, then the images, the patterns and the rules in a person's mind may support one another. That is to say, one of them may serve as a source of confirmation to the mind that it has produced one of the others correctly:

1. At any time, my mind has available within it countless images. Some of the items which make up these images are (auditory, visual or kinesthetic) echoes of words, phrases or sentences. If I use a new pattern which I am trying to learn, and if in so doing I produce something which agrees with one of these echoes, then I may feel confirmed in my use of the pattern.

2. Working in the opposite direction, I may repeat a spoken

---

[1] I use * to indicate an incorrect form.

word after someone or copy a written sentence out of a book. Or I may bring to mind – I may place on the 'worktable' (p. 29) – an auditory, visual or kinesthetic image fragment out of my long-term or permanent memory. In either case, that image fragment may be strengthened if it agrees with a pattern in which I have confidence, or weakened if it conflicts with such a pattern. I say that the image fragment 'fits,' or that it 'sounds right.' The widely-known behavioral psychologist B.F. Skinner would say that this kind of confirmation 'reinforces' the image fragment, or rather that it 'reinforces' the neurochemical activity that produced the image fragment. When he says that an activity has been 'reinforced,' he means that it will take place more readily in the future.

3. If I learn a rule about how a pattern works, then my ability to recall that rule will in the same sense be reinforced when I use it to help myself produce or understand examples of the pattern.

4. I may have been using a pattern for a while, and even using it with some success. Nevertheless, an explicit statement about the pattern may clarify it and help me to see how it relates to other patterns I have been using. A 'rule' may also carry with it a ring of academic authority. In any or all of these ways, a rule may reinforce a pattern.

In diagrammatic form, then:

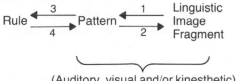

(Auditory, visual and/or kinesthetic)

Figure 1

On the basis of my experience, I believe that this diagram is valid in one way or another for all learners. 'In one way or another,' however, covers a wide range of variations, and that is where the diagram becomes particularly interesting. In some recent work with highly gifted adult learners of foreign languages, I have been astonished at how dramatic some of those variations are. They all seem to conform to the diagram, but individuals – even highly gifted individuals – differ among themselves in where their strengths lie. One of them is able to learn rules and paradigms and to hold onto them long enough so that she can produce the forms – the words and sentences – out of which she can develop a feeling for the patterns. When she produces these words and uses these patterns in genuine communication, they become parts of rich and well integrated images (3.2). In this way learning is reinforced, and at the same time acquisition (3.1) is promoted.

Another gifted individual whom I have interviewed concentrates first on massive oral repetition of words and short sentences. In so doing he builds up a stock of linguistic image fragments. The full images within which these fragments are stored are relatively impoverished and poorly integrated, but the echoes are strong enough to serve as resources for later phases of study.

This same individual then goes on to extensive practice with oral pattern drills, followed by study of rules. He does not expect to use these words and patterns in genuine conversation for a long time. In the beginning at least, almost pure learning takes place.

A third gifted individual gets her languages mostly by associating with speakers of the languages in real-life activities outside the classroom. Thus for her, the linguistic fragments are, from the beginning, parts of rich and fully integrated images. She very quickly begins to recognize patterns (including some of the most subtle ones) and to use them in her own speech. She recognizes them, however, in the way that a child recognizes a pattern in its native language, without thinking or talking *about* it. That is to say, she makes very little use of rules, and even becomes uneasy when someone tries too forcefully to urge a rule upon her. This is acquisition with very little learning.

People also differ strikingly as to the kind of linguistic image fragment – auditory, visual, or kinesthetic – that they can best hold onto and get at. If we assume that each person tends to start at the point on figure 1 where she feels most at home, then the diagram accounts for a great many quite different native learning styles. A student who is required to follow a sequence of activities which begins where she is weak and which never gets around to those areas where she is strong is likely to become annoyed and/or frustrated and/or very discouraged. In any case, her feelings of security and confidence – and ability to put herself into the activity (chapter 1) – will suffer. The lesson for you and me as teachers is *not* that we should try to teach each student in her native style; that would be impossible. But we can at least know what is going on. People often find it hard to believe descriptions of learning styles that are very different from their own. They feel that the other person is self-deceived, or is playing a joke on them. We can design our methods so that they provide opportunities for a variety of strengths. We can also remember to be specially concerned for the security of those whose learning styles harmonize least with the methods we have chosen.

4.4 'The mind,' or 'the minds'?

Up to this point, I've been talking about 'the mind' as though it were a single unit that made use of a single physical organ called 'the brain.' Actually, as you probably know, the brain consists of a right half and a left half, and these two hemispheres are quite different from each other in what they can do. They therefore make different contributions to memory and learning.

Studies of brain lateralization are relatively recent and any conclusions are only tentative. It does appear, though, that for most people the left hemisphere is the one that produces words. It is also the half that takes image fragments and performs on them such intellectual operations as abstraction, classification, labeling and reorganization. In addition, it is capable of carrying out a sequence of operations one at a time: '. . . change the *y* to *i* and then add -*es*.'

The right hemisphere, by contrast, deals in whole images, and not in the reshuffling of parts. It seems to live one moment – one gestalt – at a time, instead of ranging back and forth among past, present and future. It can recognize words and follow simple sentences, but it cannot produce language. If it sees a picture and at the same time hears from outside itself a word, it can indicate whether that word belongs with that picture, but of itself it cannot speak the word. The left hemisphere is good at analysis, while the right sees analogies more directly. The left can perform metathesis on command, while the right is at home with metaphor.

Just what all this will mean for teaching is not completely clear. We do know, however, that traditional methods in education have fed the left half of the brain much more than they have fed the right, and have also made their greatest demands on the left hemisphere. This suggests to me that at least

35

at some point in each lesson (and perhaps throughout the lesson!) we should take account of the aesthetic, holistic, uncritical but mute half of the brain as well as the rational, analytical, critical and talkative half. In chapters 6–16 you will find a few techniques which at least tend in that direction.

5 Other metaphors for memory

5.1 Introduction

In these two chapters on memory, I am giving you a series of pictures which make sense in relation to my own experience with and reading about memory, and which I find useful in dealing with my own students week by week. These pictures do not make up a single, tightly-organized theoretical model testable through laboratory experiments with control groups and all the rest. On the other hand, they *have* been developed and tested and modified and tested again, over and over, for more than thirty years. So they are the products of hard work and one kind of hard thinking, even if it hasn't been the variety of hard thinking to which we commonly give the name 'research.' After all, this is a book for people who will be dealing week after week with their own students, and who will be developing and testing and modifying their own pictures of what is happening. It is on this basis that I offer you mine.

5.2 Images and memory

The metaphor of the worktable, the wall, the stencils and the spray paint is a way of picturing some parts of what we know about human memory. It's only one picture, however. Before we go on, at the end of this chapter, to watch memory at work in some common tasks of the language classroom, let's look at one more metaphor for verbal memory. This time the individual images of simultaneously-received elements are not stencils. Instead, they are infinitesimally thin but inflexible sheets of transparent plastic. Each sheet contains all the information that was present at a given moment: verbal and nonverbal, color, size, taste, shape, weight, sound, temperature, emotional state, and all the rest. Short-term memory is not a simple tabletop, but

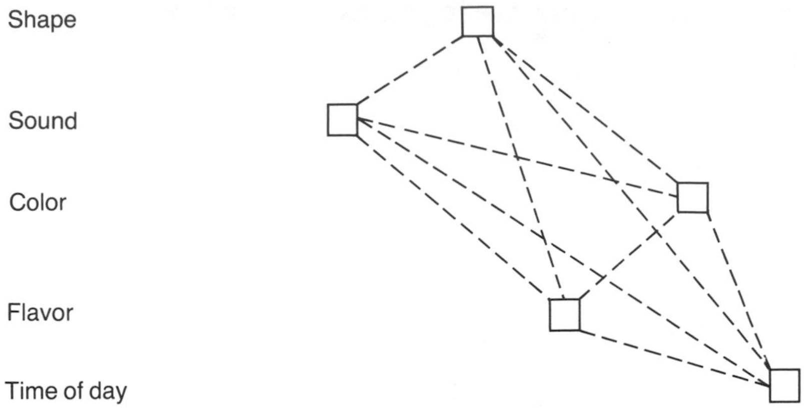

Shape

Sound

Color

Flavor

Time of day

Figure 2

a moving belt. As each sheet reaches the end of its time in STM, it falls off the end onto the top of a stack of other such sheets. If we want to retain an item from one of these sheets in STM for a longer time, we must make a copy of it and place it at the beginning of the belt again. (This is what we do when we need to remember a telephone number for a period of time but have no means of writing it down.)

Figure 2 is a vastly simplified representation of an image that includes an experience with an orange and with the word 'orange.' The broken lines stand for the fact that any one of the items can serve to bring back ('remind us of') one or more of the other items in the same image.

Figure 3 is a representation of a second experience with an orange and with the word 'orange.' The shape, flavor and color are almost the same, but not quite. Let us suppose that the verbal parts of these two experiences are identical. The two encounters took place at different times of day.

Suppose now that the person whose mind contains these images wishes to find out what the word 'orange' means. She can superimpose the two, with a result as shown in figure 4. The verbal part of the combined image is now tied to a shape-composite made up of adjacent squares, and to a color-composite, and to a flavor-composite made of other adjacent squares. Apparently the meaning has something to do with one or more of these composites. On the other hand, it is clearly unrelated to the time of day at which one hears the word.

These two images come from widely separated places in the

Shape

Sound

Color

Flavor

Time of day

Figure 3

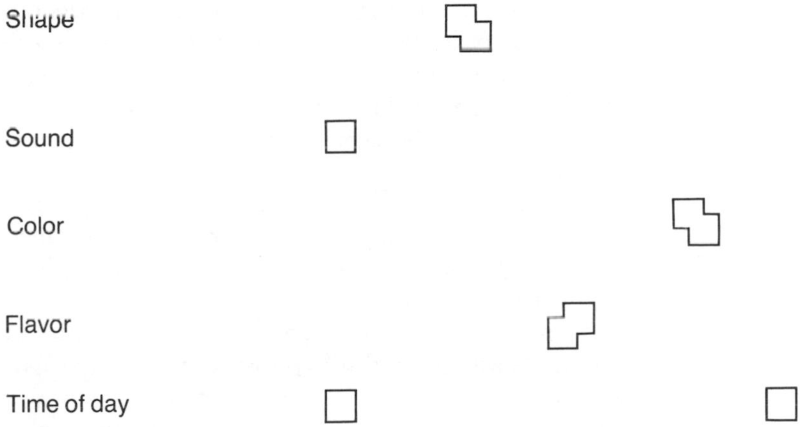

Shape

Sound

Color

Flavor

Time of day

Figure 4

chronologically ordered stack of transparencies that came off of the moving belt of STM (p. 38). How they can be withdrawn from the stack and superimposed one on the other so quickly – sometimes unintentionally, often unconsciously – is a natural mystery of memory. The fact is that it does take place, and routinely: any one item in any one image can bring back a whole stack of other images which contain either that exact item or another item that overlaps it. For example, a barking dog brings back a composite of our previous experiences with

Shape

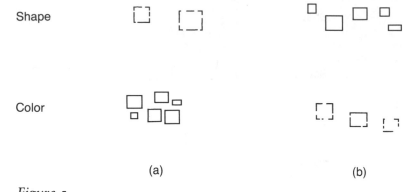

Color

(a)   (b)

Figure 5

barking dogs, or the word 'picnic' brings back images drawn from a span of many years.

Not all of the items in an image have the same sharpness or intensity. Differences of these kinds may result from differences of attention at the time the memory was formed. On the other hand, it may be that people differ from one another in which parts of an image they hold onto best. One person (figure 5a) may have a particularly good memory for colors while another (figure 5b) may be especially good at shapes but only fair at colors.

Even the relatively faint items in an image become clear if we can take the image out of the stack all by itself and hold it up to a good light. Something like this may be what happens when a hypnotist helps a witness to recover the license number of a hit-and-run car – an item to which the witness had never given her conscious attention. But hypnosis is a rare experience. Normally we pull out several images together even when we think we are looking at only one. Out of the resulting muddle we can reproduce only what stands out clearly, and we are sometimes mistaken as to whether what we reproduce came from the image that we are trying to recall, or from one or more of the other images that have come along with it.

Even when we can not reproduce some of the weaker items in an image, we can still say whether they were there if we are asked to compare them with a brand new image which contains some of the same items. So, in a common type of memory experiment, a subject might hear the following list of nouns: house, seed, stone, moon, path, egg, pen, bird, work, leaf. In this list, each of the words except one stands for an easily picturable object. In the metaphor that I am developing here, each has its own transparency (its own 'image') which contains the sound, and a written equivalent even if the list was only spoken aloud, and some kind of picture of the object. Each of these items in the image may bring back other images in which it or something very similar to it appeared. The longer the pauses between words as the list is read aloud, the more of these associated images can become available. The new image and the old ones which it brings back are superimposed on the moving belt of STM, and their composite is itself stored when its turn comes.

If now we ask the subject of the experiment to give us back as many of these words as she can, she will come up with some of them, but probably not all. If, on the other hand, we present her with a list of 20 nouns including these ten and then ask which nouns in the second list also occurred in the first, she will be able to come up with a larger number, perhaps with the entire list. *The ability to recognize is consistently better than the ability to recall.*

When the subject is asked to recall the words from this stack of transparencies, she inspects it to see what word-items stand out. She may be a person for whom the auditory part of the images is particularly clear. Or she may be someone for whom the written or the pictorial parts of the images are of better quality than the auditory items from which they orginated. If she depends mostly on the pictures, then the words that she reads back may be ones which are actually on transparencies that were brought in because they contained pictures which were like those that came from the original words. For example, this kind of person often gives 'rock' as one of the words on the list instead of 'stone.' Or the pictures brought back with 'bird' and 'egg' may combine to make the subject answer 'yes' when asked whether 'nest' was in the list. The same subject will be relatively unlikely to remember 'work' because it is harder to visualize. A different subject, who works more from sound than from pictures, may claim to recognize 'word' as having been on the list because of its auditory relationship to 'bird' and 'work.'

But the superimposition of images may be a source of help as well as a source of error. Figure 6a contains the native language (English) word 'orange.' The word brings an image that contains both *laranja* and *naranja* but both of them are too faint for clear reading. Which of the two is the correct Spanish translation? This one image is not sufficient to answer that question.

Suppose that the first image also contains a clear picture of an

Pictures

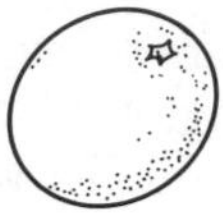

Words   *orange*   *laranja*   *naranja*

Figure 6a

Pictures

Words   *naranja*   *piña*

Figure 6b

Pictures

Words   *orange*   *laranja*   *naranja*   *piña*

Figure 6c

orange, and this picture brings back a second image (figure 6b) which also contains an orange along with a pineapple. The verbal part of this second image includes *naranja* and *piña*, but with no clear indication of which word goes with which type of fruit. Superimposing the two images, however, provides the answer to both questions (figure 6c).

As another example of how images supplement one another, consider the common task of learning to pronounce a new word in a foreign language. We are all familiar with the experience of getting part of the word but not all of it. I've frequently watched people work their way through *turuncu*, which is the Turkish word for (the color) orange. The process almost always involves a series of at least four or five wrong approximations, each followed by a new image in which the teacher provides a fresh correct model. In abbreviated and simplified form, suppose that the first image contains an orange cuisenaire rod (p. 72), but that only the first syllable was retained clearly in the linguistic portion of that image. Suppose that the second image retains the picture of the rod plus the second syllable, and the third retains the last syllable. If a learner is now shown an orange object, the object may bring back one of the images that contain the orange rod – say the first image. This image supplies the syllable *tu-* but not the rest of the word. It also brings back another image with an orange rod in it, however – perhaps the third. The learner is now able to produce *tu- -cu*. If in like manner the second image is brought back, then the whole word becomes available. If the entire process is completed *within the time span of STM*, then the learner can produce *a new image which is a composite* of the other three, and which is stored in its own right. The entire neurochemical process is 'reinforced' by success, and we say that the word has been 'learned.'

If, on the other hand, the verbal part of the second image was unclear, the learner is thereby notified that she must focus her attention the next time on the middle syllable. The process continues in this way until the whole word has been mastered as I described it in the preceding paragraph. The value in successive repetitions therefore lies less in the number of repetitions than in the selective attention which the learner gives to them, and in the partial reinforcement which she receives from them.

The concept of 'pattern' (4.3) may also be represented in this metaphor. Suppose that in our experience so far, any dot in the right-hand half of some portion of the verbal area in images has proved to have a related triangle on another transparency at

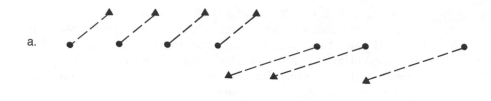

a.

b.

c.

Figure 7

some angle below it and to the left at a particular distance, while dots in the left half of the same portion of the verbal area have proved to be matched by triangles above them and to the right at some other distance. Figure 7a represents a stack of such transparencies. Now if, in our further experience, we come across a new dot in the right half of this area (figure 7b), we may guess (correctly or incorrectly) that a corresponding triangle exists (figure 7c). The pattern, then, is portrayed as a line segment of a certain length and angle operating within some definite range.

Going back to the Swahili example in chapter 4, the dots on the left side of figure 7a might be the singular nouns of the so-called *ki–vi* class, and the triangles above them are their plurals. The dots on the right side might be singular nouns of the *mu–mi* class, and the triangles their plurals. A person who hears a new noun, say *msingi* (foundation) will identify it by its prefix as belonging on the right side of the figure and so will form the plural by going southwest instead of northeast – by replacing the prefix with *mi* rather than with *vi*.

5.3 Memory in the classroom

In chapters 4 and 5, I've mentioned the results of some research on human memory. Actually, most such research has been done with people who were remembering and forgetting things in their own native languages: trying to recall things word-for-word, or trying to recall or recognize the content of what they had heard or seen. Very little has been done on how people hold onto the images, patterns and rules of a language that is new to them.

Yet it is exactly here that our interest lies. In part 2 we will look at one specific technique after another and try to understand each of them in the terms that I've been developing in these first five chapters. In the next few pages, let's see how some of these ideas might apply to foreign language study in the two general areas of the comprehension and production of individual words.

A system of language teaching that was popular in the 1920s and 1930s was the Reading Method. This was frequently a very effective method, at least between languages that share a large number of cognates and loan words. (I had my own introductions to both German and French by the Reading Method, and was very well satisfied with the results.) A conspicuous feature of Reading Method textbooks was that once a new word had been introduced, it came up again at least twice within the next 100 running words. Insofar as this feature was successful, what may have been some of the reasons for its success? What may have been going on in the students' minds? The following is my own speculation.

1. We have already seen (5.2) that any item – any picture, sound, smell, taste, etc. – has the property of bringing back whole images of which it has been a part in the past. A word is just one more kind of item, and any time we encounter it, we experience (consciously or unconsciously) whatever images it brings. These images may be more or less clear and more or less strong, depending partly on how well we know the words and partly on just what our earlier experiences were. Even a word that I have met only once will generate some kind of minimal image. Images from all of the words in a sentence (or larger context) combine to produce a meaning for the whole. Each word contributes to the interpretation of other words that are near it. Figure 8a is a vastly simplified picture of what I am trying to say. It shows a sentence made up of three words (W_1,

Figure 8a

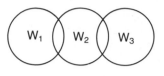

Figure 8b

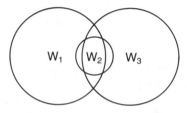

Figure 8c

W$_2$, W$_3$). The circle around each word stands for the image or composite images that it brings with it – the same kinds of thing that were pictured in greater detail in figures 2–5. In figure 8a, the images are weak or impoverished or both. The words don't support one another to make the sentence hang together. In figure 8b, the images are strong enough or rich enough so that they do support one another and produce a connected and meaningful whole. In figure 8c, W$_1$ and W$_3$ are strong enough or rich enough so that they produce the necessary coherence even without W$_2$. Under these circumstances, we say either that W$_2$ was 'redundant' or that we were able to 'get its meaning from the context.'

2. The first time I meet a new word, it can make no such contribution to the total meaning of its context. What meaning it has for me is a result of its place among other words and among the images which they have brought with them. If the sum of these contributions is great enough, and if the pattern that they generate is clear enough, I say that I have 'guessed the word from the context.' Otherwise, I may be sure only that the

word stands for 'some kind of building,' or 'a quality desirable in a pet.' Or I may look the word up in a bilingual dictionary. In any case, the new word has now become part of a new image which also contains the whole context in which it occurred, along with anything that I may have found in the dictionary. *This image is associated with neurochemical changes in my brain.* The neurochemical record remains available for a while, though it fades with the passage of time.

3. The next time I meet the same word, the same process takes place, except this time the word brings with it something of the image in 2, and so contributes to my understanding of the word itself as well as to the total context of each nearby word. *My recall of this image is at least in part a neurochemical process.* Like any neurochemical process which leads to (physical or intellectual) action, this recall process is reinforced by whatever success it meets. At the same time, I store a new image which includes this second occurrence of the new word together with the context in which I have met it.

4. The same thing happens the third time I meet the new word. This time, however, I have *two* earlier images on which I can draw. I will therefore recognize the word more readily than before, and it will also contribute more to the context of its neighbors. This increased success reinforces even more strongly the neurochemical (side of the) images which contain the word.

5. As this process is repeated, my ability to respond to the word quickly and accurately grows stronger and surer, so that I can afford to wait longer and longer between successive encounters with it. In addition, the word comes closer and closer to carrying its own weight in building the total meaning of the sentences in which it occurs. And somewhere along the way, I will meet it in one or more settings which contribute to 'acquisition' and not just to the academic type of 'learning.'

6. The timing of the successive occurrences of the word is important. If they come too close together, then I can get the meaning for the later occurrence just by using an echo that is still in my short-term memory: an echo either from the context or from my dictionary. I may have learned that the German word *Grille* means cricket. If the next occurrence of *Grille* comes just a few words after the first, I may merely play over in my head the words *Grille* = cricket, rather than having to activate the full image. If I don't activate the full neurochemical image, then it will not share in whatever reinforcement comes from success.

If, on the other hand, the occurrences of the word are *too* far apart, there is no danger of my depending on a purely verbal echo. By the same token, however, the neurochemical trace (the image) containing the information that I need may have faded so far – may have worked itself so far down into the pile – that I can't get it back readily. This is consistent with findings of the experimental psychologists who investigated the effects of 'massed' and 'distributed' practice (p. 30).

The need to have the occurrences close enough to one another can be expressed in still another word picture – one which is worth a few lines here because it has seemed to have intuitive appeal for my own students, and particularly for the ones who are least 'gifted' in languages.

Imagine a tall glass cylinder with a hole near the bottom. This cylinder represents mastery of some word. When water reaches the top of the cylinder, the word will be securely established in LTM. Now suppose that you are given a cup that holds a fifth as much as the cylinder, and are told to fill the cylinder. If you dally too long between cupfuls, you will never get the water to the top. If you add one cupful right after another, you can reach the top almost as quickly as if the cylinder didn't have a hole at the bottom.

Moreover, some cylinders have larger holes at the bottom than others: some students have much more trouble in mastering new words than others have. It is these slower students who particularly suffer from widely spaced recurrences, and who seem particularly grateful when the interval is short.

Let's turn now to the actual production of words that we have learned only recently. Not long ago, I asked a group of Swahili learners to try to think of the Swahili word for 'I didn't arrive' (*sikufika*). I didn't ask them to say the word or write it, but only to think of it. Then I asked them to tell me what went on in their heads as they put the word together. As I had thought they might, each came up with a different kind of answer. In terms that we have used in this and the previous chapter, some used images directly, while others began with only partial images and eked them out by using patterns or rules: 'I remembered the word out of a conversation we were having this morning.' 'I knew that "I didn't know" was *sikujua*, so I got it from that.' 'First I said *silifika*, but then I remembered that in the negative the past prefix is *-ku-* and not *-li-*.' and so on. To the extent that they drew on images, some relied on visual material while others seemed to get the image fragments back in audible form. This is merely additional illustration for some points that I made earlier. What is important here is that we normally have available to us two or three or even more paths – neurochemical processes – by which we might arrive at such an answer, and that some of these paths are stronger than others; that we can use the result of one of these processes to verify the result of another; and that the 'reinforcement' which a weaker path gains in this way can strengthen it just as a 'Very good!' from a teacher does.

What I said about the intervals between successive occurrences of a word in reading applies also to the occasions on which a learner is called on to produce a word that she has not yet fully acquired: if these intervals are too short, the learner can come out with the necessary performance by relying on no competence except the general ability to echo recent words. If the intervals are too long, much of the benefit of the earlier image will be lost, and each production of the new word will be almost as much work as if the word were completely new.

5.4 Conclusion

In these first five chapters, I've been trying to share with you some of the things I've found out about 'what goes on inside and among the people in a language classroom.' Any description of techniques has been incidental to that purpose. If we were planning a farm together, this would correspond to surveying the land and testing the soil and locating the sources of water. These are necessary preliminaries, but by themselves they won't produce a crop. We still need to examine hoes, plows and harrows, and to learn how to use them, and to know something about planting seed.

PART 2 SOME TECHNIQUES AND WHAT'S BEHIND THEM

6 Building auditory images: pronunciation

6.1 Introduction

All right, you say, I now see something of the *who* and *why* of my students. I understand the difference between competence and performance, and between learning and acquisition. I'm glad to have those ideas about memory and images and patterns and rules and all the rest. But I have to go into a classroom less than a week from now. What do I *do* there?

In this chapter and in chapters 7–16, we will look at nothing but techniques. Just knowing a few techniques won't get you very far, however. The trick is to fit the technique to what is going on at the moment, and for this purpose it won't be enough to *know* one technique or another. You will also need to *understand* it – to see what's behind it and how it's related to other techniques. Then you will be able to generate for yourself as many techniques as you need, and you will begin to develop an instinct for choosing rapidly and wisely among them. Let's see first how this principle can apply to the teaching of pronunciation. Then in later chapters we'll see examples of it with other kinds of activity.

6.2 Using drills to teach pronunciation

From one point of view, the most fundamental thing you teach in a language course is pronunciation. When you do so, you are helping your students to build up in their brains a very special set of models, which are composites of the audible portion of many, many memory-images (chapters 4 and 5). These models are for learners their only portable record of what the vowels and consonants and melodies and rhythms of the new language ought to sound like. In this part of your teaching, therefore, you are contributing toward a crucially important part of their linguistic competence (chapter 2).

There are several ways to approach the teaching and learning of pronunciation. Some of the newer ones are sophisticated and exciting. Let's begin, however, with one which is relatively primitive, both historically and technically, but which I think still has a place in some styles of teaching. (Some schools may even require you to use it from time to time.) This is the one in which you say a word or phrase, the students repeat it after you either chorally or individually, and then you confirm or correct what they have said. (T—teacher, C—class, S—individual student.)

> T: Good morning!
> C: Good morning!
> T: Good morning!
> C: Good morning!
> T: Good morning!
> S₁: Good morneen!
> T: MOR*ning*. Good morning!
> S₁: Good morning!

and so on.

This technique was used for some years as the first half of what was called 'Mimicry–Memorization.' The material practiced in this way was generally a dialog of some kind which the students then went on to learn by heart. 'Mimicry–Memorization' was in fact the cornerstone of the Audiolingual Method. It is less widely used today, for two reasons. One is that the memorization part, though highly effective and reasonably quick for some learners, was thoroughly unpleasant and very slow for others. The other is that both the mimicry side and the memorization side of this technique are what teachers generally call 'drills,' by which they mean that the activities are purely mechanical, and both dull and dulling to a learner's mind: at best a waste of time that could be better used in other ways, at worst a source of unproductive fatigue and a drag against motivation. If this is all there is to drills, then we should indeed avoid them.

In my work, however, I have frequent occasion to talk with individual students, both the quick ones and the slower ones, about how they learn. Many of them seem to welcome drills and to think that they are getting something useful out of them. At first I explained this to myself by saying that these students had been brainwashed by audio-lingual teachers in their secondary schools, or that they had some personal craving to be dominated, or that they were intellectually lazy and found that drills made fewer demands on their imagination or ingenuity. Over the years, however, these explanations have not convinced me. Maybe there is more to this kind of drilling than I had thought. If there is, what might it be?

One reason why some students ask for drills may be just the plain old emotional security that comes when one is engaged in a very narrowly defined task in which one knows exactly what is expected. The scope of a drill is easily explained at the beginning if necessary, but even without explanation it usually becomes clear after the first line or two just by demonstration.

There are cognitive advantages to the simplicity of a drill too, of course, and this is a second reason for using them as we learn or teach a language. The mind, using some of its parallel pathways as well as the teacher's 'right or wrong' reactions, can spot gaps in its images and inadequacies in its patterns, and work to remedy them. This is much more difficult to do while one is at the same time engaging in meaningful communication.

A third advantage to the repetitive nature of a typical drill is that you can easily conduct it in a way that establishes and maintains a steady rhythm. I don't mean necessarily the rhythm you find in a song, or the exact rhythm of a metronome, though these are possible and desirable in some kinds of drill. I do mean, however, that the steps of your technique stand out clearly from one another, and that they follow one another in an order that your students can recognize, and that they recur at some regular interval. That interval may be five seconds or less, or it may conceivably be a few minutes in length. What is essential to rhythm in this sense is that your students know without having to think about it – that they feel in their bodies – what kind of thing is going to happen and when. In maintaining a rhythm in your classroom activities, you will make several benefits available to your students. Physically, their bodies will respond to it; emotionally, it will catch them up in a feeling of security because they sense that you know what you're doing, and also because they sense that you, they and their classmates are all sharing in something that is deep and elemental; intellectually, it is economical of mental energy because the students don't have to be continuously figuring out the procedure while they are trying at the same time to work on the language. The unobtrusive use of rhythm can extend, in fact, far beyond drilling. It is one of two ideas which I have found invaluable from day to day with a wide variety of techniques.

The second idea you can apply to anything you do is that surprisingly small variations in technique can have subtle but powerful effects on how your students respond. Sometimes as you listen to your class, you know that they still need more practice on the point you are drilling. At the same time, however, you can see from their faces that they are bored with what you and they are doing together. Or perhaps only a part of the group needs additional work while the rest of the students have had all they need. Or perhaps only a few appear bored while the others are still enjoying the activity. Some find the task easy and are impatient to move ahead. Others are confused and hesitant with what they are supposed to be practicing, and so feel discouraged or embarrassed. When you teach with your eyes on your students as well as on the book, you notice that this sort of mixed reaction from a class is the rule rather than the exception. What should you do?

The best trick I have found in dealing with this kind of problem is this: modify your basic *technique* just enough so that your students will feel they are moving ahead to a new challenge. At the same time, keep the *content* of the activity pretty much the same so as not to overload those who are still having trouble with it. If you find two or more ways of handling one aspect of the technique, and two or more ways of handling a second and a third and a fourth aspect, then all of these variations will not merely add to one another – they will actually *multiply* one another. This can give you an amazingly full and flexible array of tools, and this flexibility means that each variation will now be more effective than it could have been alone. Just how much of a change will give your students that feeling of progress will of course vary from class to class and even from day to day. So you will need to govern yourself according to the reactions you are getting as you go along.

Let's turn back, then, to the mimicry drill and see what we can do with these two principles (rhythm and the variation of technique). Here are some variations in technique to which many of my own classes have responded well.

1. *Repetition by the whole class* versus *repetition by groups or rows* versus *individual repetition*. When the whole class repeats in chorus, individual students have the greatest amount of security. They can limber up their pronunciation without the prospect of being picked out as sounding somehow defective.

And because you don't stop to work with individuals at this time, you can maintain a relatively rapid, very stable and very physical rhythm.

In group repetition, you are listening to from three to six voices at once. This has the advantage of preserving a large degree of individual security while at the same time allowing you to begin to hear how individuals are doing. The goal has now begun to move away from limbering up and toward shaping up. One suggestion: have your students do their group repetitions in a voice which is firm *but not loud*. In this way the more timid ones will be less likely to be drowned out by the more confident ones. Your own ear, also, will not be over-loaded. And the whole exercise will make more economical use of energy and voices. Another suggestion: if at all possible, move about the room from group to group and stand alongside each group as you listen to it. If you look past the group rather than at it, both you and they will be better able to concentrate on the sound and to minimize any element of interpersonal confrontation.

Similarly in dealing with individual repetitions, it's a good idea to concentrate the student's attention and your own on the sound rather than on interpersonal confrontation. You may therefore look in his direction, but unless you have some special reason to check the position of his lips you won't stare directly at him. For the same reason, you probably won't walk from one student to another at this stage.

The most important feature of individual repetition in this technique is that the student wants to know how close each of his attempts was to the target. You can let him know in words, of course: 'Very good!' or 'No, that's not it,' or 'Not quite, but better than last time.' But using words for this purpose takes time and breaks up the rhythm. It also adds to that atmosphere of evaluation and confrontation that I mentioned in the preceding paragraph. I recommend that you work out a system of hand gestures and facial expressions for getting this information to your students. If you are consistent in the ways you use these signals, your students will catch onto them quickly. Your using gestures here instead of words need not take anything away from the human quality of your interchanges with your students. The gestures can become a shared code, and the very sharing of the code can even contribute to solidarity. As in so many of the things you do, your body language and your general demeanor will go far toward determining how silent gestures will be received.

2. *Calling on students (or groups) in fixed order* versus *calling on them in random order*. Again, the first alternative is the one that provides the students with the greater degree of security. The second has the advantage of keeping them on their toes. Some experts recommend doing one, while others prescribe in the opposite direction. In my experience, there's a place for each. Students don't *always* need maximum security. After you've gotten into a drill and they see what it's about, most classes will be ready for the more challenging alternative. But as I said at the beginning of this chapter, don't go by what I say here. Go by what you are hearing from your own class at the moment, and by the looks that you see on your students' faces.

Another variation in this aspect of drilling is to *shift from one fixed order to another*: clockwise to counterclockwise; calling on students from the front to the back of rows, then from back to front; calling on every second or third student, and so on. In following any of these patterns, you can pretend to overlook someone. Then everyone will be in (a simple kind of) suspense to see whether you will rectify your 'oversight.' Or you can call on students in random order, looking at no-one in particular until a second or two after you have given the cue or prompt to which they are to respond. Some teachers look at one student while saying the word or sentence and then point suddenly at some other student to do the actual repetition. Some good teachers that I know find that this sort of thing simply does not fit in with their classroom style; for others, it is a small way of being mildly playful with their students, and they make excellent use of it.

3. *Students' books closed* versus *students' books open*. Here's another place where some experts recommend in one direction and some in the other. Again, I think there's a time and a place for each alternative. The first requires the students' ears to work, rather than letting them hear what their eyes tell them to hear. For example, I was once told, and quite insistently, that the Portuguese word for 'good' ends with the consonant *m* as in English 'home.' In fact the word ends with a nasalized vowel, just like the French *bon*. But my friends' ears, all through their many months in Portugal, had 'heard' that *m* because their eyes had seen the spelling, which is *bom*.

The second of these alternatives has the advantages of leaving some students much less anxious, and of providing a visible input to balance and corroborate the audible side of the drill. I know two extraordinarily effective teachers who choose this alternative and with it establish a remarkable, reassuring rhythm that produces consistently superior results.

There's a third alternative, of course, which I've often used with great satisfaction: *the students' books are open, but the students look away from them as much as they can*. Once again you yourself, as you observe your students' reactions, will have to determine when it's time to do what.

4. *Two or three repetitions per student (or group)* versus *only one repetition* before going on to the next student (or group). A student will find it helpful to compare the results of consecutive tries rather than having to wait a minute or two between turns. On the other hand, giving only one repetition per customer undoubtedly livens up the rhythm and allows each one less time in which to let his mind wander before you call on him again. If you as teacher keep these alternatives clearly separated in your mind, and move crisply from one to the other, you will enhance your students' feeling of firm direction and frequent progress.

5. *Slow tempo* versus *fast tempo*. The advantages of each of these alternatives are obvious. I only list them here as a reminder that they are available and usually effective in giving to students the feeling that there has been a significant change in what they are doing.

6. Tone of voice: *neutral* versus *mysterious or mischievous* versus *triumphant or emphatic.*

7. Loudness: *barely audible* versus *normal* versus *oratorical.*

You may be able to think of other dimensions. So far, however, we have $3\times2\times3\times2\times2\times3\times3$ alternatives. The arithmetical product is 648. A few combinations are self-contradictory, of course. For example, 'choral repetition by the whole class' cannot go along with 'random versus fixed order of recitation.' Even so, we are left with some *hundreds of perfectly workable combinations*. Let me emphasize once more that coming up with such a large number is not just a sterile *tour de force* on my part. I hope that these last few paragraphs have helped you to *see techniques in terms of their components*, and that with practice you will become very nimble at shuffling these components into new combinations as you see need for them. Then they will work for you. You will not be a slave either to someone else's prescriptions or to your own unexamined habits.

6.3 Mimicry

These last few pages have been about drills in general, and will apply equally to much of what you will find in chapters 7–14. Let's go back now and pick up again our discussion of the most widely-used technique for teaching pronunciation, which we interrupted on p. 51. This technique places its principal emphasis on what in chapter 2 I called learning. That is to say, it concentrates on identifying for students a number of specific points at which they could do better, and on providing them with corrections. A correction is, in effect, a new image into which you as teacher place an example of what the learner ought to sound like. But remember that the total image also contains many other items including your tone of voice, as well as the learner's own deepest feelings about sounding like the correction.

Teachers and textbook writers who have relied on this technique have urged students to 'mimic – don't just repeat.' 'Mimicry' in this sense meant 'doing the same thing you would do if your were trying to copy or make fun of the accent of a foreigner who was speaking your own language.' For some reason, however, the injunction to mimic was only partially successful in producing native-like pronunciation.

The principal reason, I suspect, was this: genuine mimicry takes place only with certain configurations of motivation, both negative and positive. Negatively, if I am to mimic successfully, I must not feel any reluctance to sound like the person I am mimicking. Positively, I must desire either to ridicule that person or to become more like her or him. In either case, I must feel a certain amount of social power as I mimic. As 'Mim–Mem' was too often used in the classroom, however, it made either of these motivations relatively difficult for anyone, and impossible for some. In fact, emphasis was on trying to do things 'right' enough so that one would not need further corrections (further 'new models'). All power was with the teacher.

What we didn't think about then was that there are at least four ways of saying a word or sentence after someone else. One is *perfect personal mimicry*, in which what one says is absolutely indistinguishable from the original: the model's wife, listening from the next room, would not be certain whether it was her husband speaking, or someone else. A few people are good at this kind of mimicry, but it is of no practical interest to us as language teachers.

The second alternative is *perfect linguistic mimicry*. Here, one captures all of the nuances of the original, but in one's own voice. One would not be able to pass for the model himself, but one might be taken for a native of the same town. This is the stated goal of 'Mimicry–Memorization.'

In the third kind of saying-after, one misses some of the nuances, so that one is identifiable as a foreigner. Nevertheless one makes all of the distinctions that are necessary for keeping words apart in the foreign language (what in chapter 17 are called 'phonemic' distinctions). That is, one pronounces *law* different from *raw*, but the exact quality of the *l* and/or the *r* may be definitely foreign. Even in words for which no minimally contrasting word exists (e.g. *draw*, for which the counterpart *dlaw* is impossible in English), the *r* is clearly some kind of *r*, and not an *l*. This *'phonemically accurate' imitation* is sometimes cited as the highest realistic goal for the everyday teacher with an everyday class.

In the fourth and last kind of saying-after, the student uses nothing but her native sound system. The result is an *undiluted foreign accent*: I teenk joo are rrigh. Of course no teacher wants to hear this fourth kind of imitation. Few if any students would consciously choose it either. Why then do so many of them end up with some blend of the third and fourth alternatives? I think that very little of the answer to this question lies in sheer laziness. While it may be true that some of us have 'better ears' than others, I doubt that the greatest part of the answer lies in differences of genetic endowment. One important part, I suspect, is the communicative function of the nuances of pronunciation – those aspects of speech which do *not* serve to distinguish words like *law* and *raw*, or *ship* and *sheep*. These nuances carry information which is not lexical but social: Where did the speaker grow up? With whom does she associate regularly? With whom would she like her hearers to identify her? These minor phonetic details are an ideal medium through which a speaker can verify with her own ears her private image of herself, and project to others the image that she wants them to receive. The fourth kind of saying-after therefore offers a source of emotional security which is diminished in phonemically accurate repetition, and is totally absent in genuine mimicry.

The nuances of pronunciation, therefore, and even some of the necessary, meaning-bearing distinctions of a new language, will be taken in and stored and assimilated only as part of a total human experience in which sounding unlike oneself and like someone else somehow feels acceptable. In this respect the development of good competence in pronunciation is much more like acquisition (chapter 3) than it is like learning.

6.4 Minimal pairs

After Mimicry–Memorization, the use of 'minimal pairs' is perhaps the most primitive technique for the teaching of pronunciation. And it is indeed a technique for 'teaching' in the narrow sense of promoting 'learning' (chapter 3) but doing very little directly for 'acquisition.' Even if you are concentrating on acquisition, however, you can use minimal pair drills occasionally in order to sharpen your students' hearing of some of the sounds that they are in the process of acquiring.

A minimal pair is a pair of words or longer expressions which differ in their meanings, but which sound exactly alike except at one point: *du* and *doux* in French, *Stadt* and *Staat* in German, *pero* and *perro* in Spanish, *black bird* and *blackbird* in English. The object is to select minimal pairs that illustrate a difference which is important in the language you are teaching, but which is unimportant or even nonexistent in your students' native language(s). Minimal pairs not only sharpen hearing; they also dramatize the importance of learning to control the sounds that they illustrate: 'If you don't get this pair of vowels straight, you may someday tell someone that you came to this country on a big *sheep*!'

A basic procedure for using minimal pairs conforms to the classical audiolingual formula 'Hearing before Speaking, Speaking before Reading, Reading before Writing.' It goes as follows:

1. Pronounce the pair of words several times, always in the same order:

> ship.   sheep.
> ship.   sheep.
> ship.   sheep.

Let the students try to hear the difference for themselves first. As you pronounce the words, it's a good idea to follow two very practical rules. First, leave a couple of seconds after the first member of each pair, and a little longer after the second member. The two-second pause allows the students time to play the word over in their minds and so to work with it in short-term memory (chapter 4). The longer pause marks the boundary between successive voicings of the pair. Without it the student, who hasn't yet learned to hear the difference between the two sounds, may quickly lose track of which is which. This can be upsetting emotionally and unproductive linguistically.

The second practical rule is to pronounce each word as though it stood by itself, with the intonation that you would use at the end of a sentence. An English example is:

sh\ip   sh\eep

and not:

sh/ip, sh\eep

2. Pronounce the pair at least ten more times, but this time in random order, and occasionally pronouncing the same word twice:

        ship   sheep
        ship   ship
        sheep   ship

After each pair the students reply in unison 'Same' or 'Different.' You then give the correct answer in a quiet, matter-of-fact voice and go on immediately to the next pair. Or instead of the spoken answers, provide each student and yourself with two squares of colored cardboard. In the context of this step, holding up one color means 'Same' and holding up the other means 'Different.' In this way, the students hear nothing during the drill except the sounds that they are learning to distinguish. Their security is increased because there is no chance of their neighbors over-hearing them as they give a wrong answer. And you can keep track more accurately of just who is having trouble with what.

3. Pronounce one of the words at a time. The class replies with a one-word translation, or with 'One' or 'Two,' so that they commit themselves as to which word they thought you said. As in step 2, you give the correct answer in a quiet and matter-of-fact way and go on to the next item. If you use colored cards, assign one of them to 'sheep' and the other to 'ship.'

In all of the steps of this drill, but especially in these first three steps where the class is responding in unison, try for a gentle but very clear physical rhythm.

4. Comment very briefly on the physical nature of the difference between the two words. (This is the kind of information with which we will be concerned in chapter 18.) Then go through one or more of steps 1–3 again to allow the students to use this new knowledge as they listen.

5. Reverse roles in step 3, with individual students speaking the words and you telling them which ones you hear. When you're not sure which word you're hearing, reply '1½.' You may

find it smoother to point to large numbers on the blackboard rather than giving your replies orally.

6.5 'Acquisitional' techniques for pronunciation

I have said that 'Mim–Mem,' the widely used technique for teaching pronunciation, depends principally on learning, and that one of the essential components of acquisition is an emotional one. Other components of acquisition are the meeting of new material in contexts where it is necessary but is not the principal focus of attention; the opportunity to listen for a while and build up passive competence before beginning active performance; and the possibility of participating meaningfully in what is going on without 'making errors.' The following are a few techniques which share some of these characteristics of acquisition.

Selective listening

Listening has sometimes been described as a 'passive' skill along with reading, in contrast to the 'active' skills of speaking and writing. More recently, however, we are coming to see that reading and listening are 'passive' only in the sense that the reader or listener is not putting out a stream of language which other people can see or hear. Normal reading and listening outside of the language classroom as well as inside it do involve constant mental activity. During the years in which a child is acquiring its first language, no-one tries to give very much structure to this inner activity. There is, after all, plenty of time. You get some of this same effect to the extent that you use the target language not only in the lesson materials themselves, but also in giving classroom instructions and in talking about what is happening as it happens. But in the weeks and months – the few hundred hours – that your students are with you, you may want to structure their inner activity as listeners more than a parent tries to structure the inner activity of a listening child.

Begin, then, with a recording of one or two people who are really using the language: a telephone conversation, a fragment of a news broadcast or of a dramatic program from radio or television, for example, or a conversation between yourself and another speaker of the language you are teaching. Most new language courses with a listening component now provide some authentic listening material such as airport or station announcements. Whatever the material, your goal is to structure, in multiple ways, your students' experience with this text which was not written or spoken with language students in mind. The general formula for doing this is: require them to respond to the text in some way(s) that can be seen or heard, but which do not allow them to attempt pronunciation. The fragment should be long enough so that there is no question of their remembering it entire, and short enough so that they can hear it several times in the course of 20 or 30 minutes and respond to it in a variety of ways. Here are some sample instructions to get you started:

1. Listen and form in your mind a picture of what the speaker or speakers look like. Then compare your mental picture with someone else's.

2. Listen and then discuss *very briefly* with other listeners how the speakers seem to feel about what they are saying.

3. Listen and tap with your finger each time there is a pause.

4. Listen and lift your hand slightly when the speaker's voice goes up.

5. Here is a list of two to five words. How often does each occur in the recording?

6. What words or conspicuous suffixes or prefixes recur in the recording?

7. Pick out examples of specific vowels or consonants. (This can be repeated for each of several sounds.)

8. Which of these sequences of words occurs in the recording:

> *call him up*, or *call a plumber?*
> *right way*, or *right away?*
> *closing sale*, or *clothing sale?*

You can vary the differences for which the students are to listen, from gross ones as in the first example to extremely fine ones as in the last.

Selective production

In most techniques for systematic work on pronunciation, the teacher not only monopolizes 'control,' but also exercises almost all of the 'initiative.' These techniques therefore contribute to the student's feeling of being 'powerless and constantly evaluated' (chapter 1). To the extent that you can share initiative with your students, you will be able to minimize that feeling. At least as important, you will increase their feeling of personal investment in what they are doing from moment to moment, and will also increase the likelihood that what they are doing fits exactly into what they know and do not know and are ready for at any given time.

Here is a procedure that maximizes student initiative in working on pronunciation, yet without allowing the activity to get out of control:

1. Select a list of three to ten words in the language you are teaching.

2. Write these words in a single column on the blackboard. Opposite each word write its equivalent in the students' native language. (If your students come from many different language backgrounds, simply number the words instead of translating them.)

3. Let the students take turns in working with the words. If the class is small, everyone can play at once. If it is large, select six 'players' from different parts of the room. In order to avoid irrelevant uncertainty about who is to speak and when, the players rotate turns in some fixed order.

4. Each turn consists of three parts: (a) The player *either* tries to pronounce one of the words from the list *or* reads aloud its native language equivalent (or its number). (b) *In either case*, you respond by pronouncing the word in the language you are teaching. For the moment, you give no indication of whether or where there were any errors. (c) The same player *either* repeats the word after you *or* remains silent. You still withhold any indication of correctness.

5. One player takes two consecutive turns. This allows her to try out in her second turn anything that she thinks she learned in her first. She may use the same word in both turns, or she may choose a different word the second time. It is then the turn of the next player.

6. After each player has had three or four pairs of turns, point out *to the group as a whole* whatever sounds are still causing trouble. Then give each player a few more turns in which to try to profit from what you have told them.

In this technique you give the initiative to your students at three points. In 4a, they must choose among the words in the list, and must also choose whether to try the foreign language or to stick to the safety of their native language.

In 4c, they again have the option of attempting the foreign pronunciation or of remaining silent. Notice also that you are giving them psychological support in two ways, not just one: by avoiding a judgmental, 'correcting' manner in 4b, but also by keeping them informed in 6.

I have found that this technique provides enough personal security so that even the weaker students quickly move away from the linguistic security of the easiest options in 4a and 4c. At the same time, it provides enough flexibility so that faster and slower students can work smoothly side by side, each at a rate appropriate for her.

In a simple modification of this technique the students work not from a list of words, but from the sentences of a story or a dialog. Each student reads aloud a word or phrase of her own choosing. In this way they control the length of what they try to do. Your basic response, as in 4b, is a clear and supportive repetition of what they have said.

If you find your students are consistently choosing to repeat after you in 4c, and if the activity has settled into a solid rhythm, you can modify your basic response (4b) by speeding up your rate of speech. If you do so gradually, and in the spirit of a shared game rather than a demand, your students will begin to copy you almost without noticing it. When they do notice it, they may find that they are performing well beyond anything they would have attempted on their own. This modification of the basic technique does, however, require you to monitor very closely both the linguistic performance and the emotional reactions of your students. Don't try it until you've had a few months' experience as a teacher.

6.6 Where should you stand?

As you have read my descriptions of these techniques for helping people with pronunciation, you have probably visualized yourself as a teacher conducting the activities from the front of the classroom. They will indeed work that way, but there are two more choices that you may want to consider. One is, 'How close should I stand to the student I am working with at the moment?' The second is, 'Should I stand where the student(s) can see me?'

In answering the first question, most of us assume that we should stand close enough for the student to see us, but not so close that we invade her personal space. I took this for granted until one day when I was watching a Pakistani teach Urdu pronunciation to some native speakers of English. When one of the learners had persistent difficulty with a particular sound, he very gently moved until his mouth was about 15 centimeters in front of her left shoulder – much closer than she was accustomed to being approached by strangers. Then, after pausing for a second or two, he said the word *once, very softly*. She immediately pronounced the sound correctly, and had much less difficulty with it from then on. I've seen the same trick work a number of times since then, and have used it myself, but I can't explain it. Perhaps a sound which originates from that close is treated the same as a sound that originated from within oneself, and so is exempted from the allergic reaction which we sometimes have against that which comes from outside. Perhaps the location of the teacher's mouth, close to the learner's left ear and clearly removed from its normal conversational location, caused the learner to process the sound mainly through the right hemisphere of her brain, as a non-speech noise.

In one style of teaching that I have sometimes used, I provide models for individual repetition while I am standing behind the student, with my mouth just a few centimeters from her head. This generally produces repetitions that are at least as accurate as any that I get when I'm standing in front of people, and sometimes considerably better. I also sometimes give models for group repetition while standing at the back of the room. This practice has often been the subject of comment from students. One student out of perhaps five or six dislikes it because 'I need all the information I can get, from watching you as well as listening to you.' It is true that we can see the lip position of a speaker, but that is about all we can normally see about how a sound is formed, and as we will see in chapter 18, the essential features of the articulation of most sounds are not ordinarily visible at all. So this kind of student is clearly mistaken in complaining that she is being deprived of important articulatory data when we stand behind her. I suspect that what she *is* craving is a chance to take in a fuller image, including visual cues about timing and facial expression. Actually, most students seem to prefer having me behind them so that they can respond to the sound as sound without at the same time searching my face for signs of approval or disapproval.

6.7 Conclusion

This has been the first of a series of chapters about techniques. I have therefore used it as a vehicle for introducing the principles of rhythm in classroom activity, and of subtle systematic variation in basic techniques so as to maintain that rhythm. Together, these two principles can operate, largely outside your students' awareness, to build their confidence in themselves and in you. Now let's go on and see how these same principles can work in other aspects of your teaching.

7 Memorization: building usable composite images for meaningful material

7.1 Introduction

Good pronunciation is only a start. It provides your students with a more widely acceptable and more intelligible medium in which to mold what they say. That's all it can do, and that by itself can even be dangerous. (A French teacher once warned me, 'If you try speaking French in France you'll annoy a lot of people because you pronounce so well but know so little.') So your students must also, somehow, learn *what* to pronounce. They must hold onto as much as possible from the words, grammatical rules and whole sentences that they have met in your classroom. Only those things that they still retain at their fingertips after they have left you will be effective resources for them to use in life outside the classroom.

What we teachers are ultimately concerned about, then, is helping our students to retain language which they can use in an appropriate context. That is what this chapter is about. Memorization is one conspicuous road to retention, and the road at which we shall look most closely here. It is only one such road, however; if we ignore the others we limit our students' progress.

As I shall use the term 'memorization' in this book, it means working on a body of material until one is able to reproduce it word for word on demand. In this sense, the word is applied to a number of activities: memorization of dialogs, memorization of tables of inflected forms of nouns, verbs and so forth, memorization of monologs such as anecdotes or poems, and memorization of vocabulary lists. I'll describe techniques for each of these later in the chapter.

Many teachers do not expect their students to memorize material word for word although they would expect them to be able to reproduce key expressions and certainly to memorize vocabulary. Therefore the techniques for memorization of dialogs, paradigms and monologs which I describe here and which have been successful in my classrooms and very useful in much of my own learning would not necessarily be found in every classroom today. You and these teachers may ask: 'But why talk about memorization at all? Haven't you said that retention comes naturally when a student is involved in the right way with enough samples of the language?' My answer is, *Naturally*, yes. But naturally often means *slowly*. For many people slowly means discouragement and frustration. It also places a limit on how much the student can get in a course of fixed length. Finally, it means in the short run at least that the degree of correctness in speaking and writing will be reduced. For people who don't mind doing it, memorization can be a learning activity which greatly expedites the kinds of experience which promote acquisition (chapter 3).

Memorized material is useful in two ways. Some whole sentences can be used exactly as they stand: 'How much is this?' and 'I'm afraid it's time to go' are obvious examples. Other sentences are much less likely to come up in real-life conversation, but may still serve as handy models for what students may want to say in later years. A student whose memory places at his disposal 'Can you tell me where the snack bar is?' will be less likely in real life to say the incorrect 'Can you tell me where is the post office?' or the correct but abrupt 'Where is the post office?' And he'll probably come out with 'Can you tell me where the post office is?' a lot more smoothly than he would have otherwise.

Before we go on to look at some of the techniques that help in the process of memorization, it will be worthwhile to look at just what is involved. Most of us, I suppose, had the experience as schoolchildren of being told to 'go home and memorize this poem for tomorrow.' When on the following day we wrote the poem out (for better or for worse) under the eye of the teacher or (terrifying experience!) stood to take our turn at trying to say it aloud, we learned one indisputable fact about memorization: Some of us are much, much better at it than others! For many of us, that was all we learned about it. It was some mysterious process at which different people had different degrees of ability.

And that is just where we were wrong! You don't have to talk for very long with very many people about this sort of task before you realize that memorization is not one simple process, but several complex ones. The process that one person finds easy, obvious and effective will seem to the next person to be awkward, hopeless and bizarre. We do not have space here to go into detail about any of these processes which lead to memorization. It is, however, important for you as teacher to be at least aware of a few of the ways in which people differ in this respect.

Perhaps the most important factor in determining whether people succeed in this task is their attitude toward the undertaking. Some people find memorizing easy, and may even do it just for fun. Some memorize things *inadvertently* after hearing them a few times. (I tend to be one of those.) Many consider memorization to be hard work, mildly onerous, but something they can do if they have sufficient reason to. Some – including at least a few who *can* do it fairly easily – find it intensely distasteful. And a few suffer physical symptoms – sweaty palms, trembling hands, stomach pain, etc. – when asked to commit a text to memory.

Second, people also differ sharply with respect to the mechanisms that they use in reciting a memorized poem. Some rely on an auditory image: they simply say aloud the sounds that they can hear in their brains. Others read from written images of words in their minds – even if they have only heard the poem and never seen it in printed form. Some draw heavily on their recollection of pictures and emotions that the poem generated in their minds. Some benefit greatly from writing the poem out in their own hand.

Third, people vary in the strategies that they use in memorizing. Some work through a poem line by line, beginning at one end and working straight through to the other. Some people go at it quite differently, reading the poem all the way through a few times, memorizing first those parts that prove to be easiest, and then filling in the rest around those nuclei.

What all of this means for you as teacher, then, is that for memorization activities you'll be well advised not to rely on just one narrow technique which you have chosen (consciously or not) because it is consistent with what has worked best for your own memorization. You might better employ two or more techniques for the same text, or else employ a single technique which is rich enough so that different learners can react to it in their own ways.

7.2 Techniques for memorizing dialogs

Most of the so-called audiolingual courses base each of their early lessons on a dialog. The dialog is a sample of how the language is used. In the strategy of the audiolingual system, the student first 'overlearns' the dialog. 'Overlearning' means not merely memorizing; it means memorizing so thoroughly that one is able to recite the whole very rapidly almost without thinking about it. In later steps, the student examines selected points of grammar that are illustrated in the dialog, goes through a series of drills on these points, and finally uses the new material in genuine or simulated communication. Absolute mastery of the 'basic dialog' is therefore the very cornerstone of this approach. The original and most widely used technique for laying this cornerstone is called Mimicry–Memorization (Mim–Mem).

Mimicry–Memorization

Mim–Mem is an elaboration of the massed repetition technique that we have already looked at in connection with pronunciation. It goes something like this:
 1. Establishing acceptable pronunciation.
a) Let the students hear the whole conversation a time or two.
b) Teach pronunciation of any new words in the first sentence, following the procedure outlined in chapter 6.
c) Have the students repeat the *last* part of the first sentence, following the same procedure, e.g. 'outdoors.'
d) When they can do that satisfactorily, add the word or two that came just before the end, e.g. 'to eat outdoors.' Continue with this kind of 'backward buildup' until you reach the beginning and the students are repeating the entire sentence: 'liked to eat outdoors,' 'always liked to eat outdoors,' 'I've always liked to eat outdoors.' Go on and build up each sentence in this way until the dialog is complete.
e) Let the students listen again to the entire dialog. This gives them an opportunity to take a look at the forest through which they were working their way one tree at a time in step 1d.
 2. Divide the class into groups. Have each group repeat after you the lines from one side of the dialog. In this way the groups will sound as though they are conversing with each other:
 Group 1: I've always liked to eat outdoors.
 Group 2: Yes, isn't this a nice picnic?
 and so on.

3. In the same way, have individuals repeat after you the roles in the dialog.

4. Have pairs of individuals try to take the roles from memory. It may be necessary to start with the last two lines and have several pairs of students do them. Then have them do the last four lines, the last six lines and so on until they can do the whole dialog. Or start at the beginning and work forward to the end. The reason why I like to work backward is that the learner is always moving from less familiar to more familiar material. In this way she is more likely to be left with a feeling of fluency.

As you follow this procedure, there are several well-known options open to you. The choice between single and double repetitions is one that is often listed. As with the basic procedure for pronunciation, the choice between fixed and random order of calling on students can be both/and rather than either/or. Variations of speed and loudness are again effective ways of providing a change of pace and a sense of progress without introducing new difficulties. Variations in tone of voice – plain or dramatic or emphatic – are even more important here than they were in working on pronunciation. The reason why this is so goes back to the picture of short-term memory as a worktable from which new items either do or do not get transferred to long-term memory. Changes in your tone of voice can contribute much toward the amount of intensity that is needed for that purpose. To change the figure of speech just a bit, each such variation of a single sentence gives a slightly different image of it, just as a pair of cameras placed a few centimeters apart produce slightly different pictures of a single object. These two pictures, seen together, produce a three-dimensional image in the viewer's brain. In the same way, apparently, two or more different renditions of a sentence (or word, or poem) produce a result which is richer as well as more likely to stick to the LTM wall that we were talking about in chapter 4.

There are at least two other options which you will find handy in this procedure. One is to build a long sentence up beginning not with the last of its words, but with its most salient word. The other is to allow – and, in fact, to *enforce* – a few seconds of silence between your voice and your students' repetitions. This silence will allow them to listen to the material over once or twice while it is still in STM, and begin to do their own work on it. The work they do will help it to stick in LTM.

There are of course several ways in which you can supplement this basic procedure. The use of pictures is one. Having students stand up and act the dialog out with as many gestures as possible is another. Both involve the student more than the basic procedure does, and they enrich the strictly verbal images by adding components from other sensory channels. These supplements are more effective with some dialogs than with others. You will have to be the judge.

One of the best-known facts about memory is that one item can be brought back by some other item with which it has been associated in the past (see chapter 5). The basic procedure that I have been describing works by forming a line of such associations. In the example that we used earlier, the student is first caused to say 'outdoors.' Then, while that word is still reverberating in his STM, he is led to say 'to eat outdoors.' When in future practice of this dialog he says 'to eat,' the word 'outdoors' will then pop into his mind to follow it. In the same way, 'liked' will call forth 'to eat,' and so on. The chain of associations becomes stronger every time it is repeated and the student is rewarded by knowing he has done it right.

This, then, is how the standard audiolingual technique of 'Mimicry–Memorization' moves new material from STM to LTM. Once the material is in LTM, the audiolingual method has other ways of trying to get it into PM, but I will not list them here.

If your students need to establish their pronunciation before they memorize, you may want to use one or more of the techniques in chapter 6.

Memorizing in 3-D

The technique that I have already described for memorization places heavy emphasis on the students' oral *production* of the sentences they are trying to master, as contrasted with *comprehension* of them. A second technique for memorizing dialogs also requires students to produce the words of the dialog aloud, but it involves a wider range of the students' faculties and demands greater concentration. Some teachers will prefer it for this reason.

This second technique needs a number of small, easily movable and visually neutral objects. The best thing I've found for this purpose is my old standby, the boxful of cuisenaire rods. They are wooden or plastic blocks one square centimeter in cross section and one to ten centimeters in length. Each length has its own distinctive color. Even if you don't use them for dialogs, I recommend that you get some for yourself. They are compact, portable and relatively inexpensive, but they are the most versatile teaching aid I know of at any price.

The technique consists of building a word-by-word replica of the dialog or other text to be learned, using the rods. The students then read aloud from the rods as you point to them. Some of the choices open to you in using this technique are:

1. Use actual three-dimensional rods on a tabletop; or use pieces of transparent colored plastic with an overhead projector; or use colored rectangles on a flannelgraph; or use colored chalk on a blackboard.

2. Prepare the replica yourself ahead of time; or build it one word at a time as you work with the class; or have the students build it themselves as you watch. If the text is written on the blackboard at the beginning of the process, words can be erased one at a time and replaced on the table by rods. Choose rods so that the length/color indicates something about the part of speech of the word it is replacing, or the length of that word in syllables.

3. Build the students' ability to read from the text by starting with the most important or conspicuous words; or start at the beginning and build the text one word at a time to the end; or start at the end and build it backward until you reach the beginning; or let the students say which word *they* want to start with.

4. As you point to each rod, you allow any and all students who recognize it to say the word that it stands for; or you call on one student at a time.

5. You point slowly to one word at a time; or you sweep your pointer dramatically over a whole phrase or sentence at a time.

6. Slide together, so that they touch one another, any words which seem to belong in a single breath-group; or have your students do so.

7. Remove one rod at a time and have the students call out the word that it stood for. Write these words on the blackboard and thus restore the complete text to written form. Or have this done by a student who is allowed to write only what he hears from others.

This technique is extraordinarily efficient for memorizing the words of texts up to 100 words in length. Its effectiveness apparently comes from the amazing degree of concentration which it produces in students. Some of the features which may contribute to this concentration are: (1) the silence of the teacher; (2) the clear simple visual impact of the rods (or other colored objects); (3) the absence of need to remember the number of words or the overall organization of the text; (4) a visible and tangible reference point for each word during the process of memorization.

If you feel that the students need further work in order to polish their intonation or phrasing, you may want to follow this technique with a few minutes of choral and individual repetition of the kind that I described in chapter 6.

Active listening

Both of the memorization procedures that I have described so far require the students to produce the words of the text immediately. In this third technique, you allow them to listen to the text several times before they try to reproduce it orally. Their listening is anything but passive, however. Each time you read the text through, you give them something a little different to do with it. You may want to use some or all of the following instructions. (Perhaps you will think of additional variants.)

1. *'Listen to the text, paying attention only to the rise and fall of my voice.'* One value of this instruction is that the students may actually notice the rise and fall of your voice. Another effect may be that they follow the meaning of the text better than if they had been straining to understand it. This first instruction at the same time relieves them of *responsibility* for understanding the text and also gives them a plausible task to distract them from *trying* to understand.

2. *'As you listen this time, pick out any words or parts of the text which are unclear to you.'* At the end of this step, answer questions about meaning, but not about grammar. The only purpose here is to be certain that the meaning is clear in their minds before going on to the next steps. Incidentally, the discussion and explanation that take place at this time can become oral practice of the very highest quality: people are asking questions because they really want the answers, yet the vocabulary is drawn almost entirely from a source which will be available for further reference.

3. *'Now listen and try to form in your mind a very clear and detailed picture of what the text is saying. I'll pause for a few seconds after each sentence.'* This is an opportunity for the students to confirm and enrich the new meanings while your

explanations from the second step are still fresh in their minds.

4. *'I'll read a little faster this time. Look again at the picture in your mind and see whether you want to make any changes in it.'* The unstated purpose of this step is to allow the image to become more coherent, and better integrated within itself.

5. *'I'll be silent for 15 seconds. During this time, look once again at the image you have formed.'* The purpose of the steps which follow will be to weld together as closely and as tightly as possible the form of the text and its meaning. Clarity and stability of the image are therefore essential. Otherwise steps 6–9 will be nothing but unproductive play with echoes.

6. *'As I read the text this time, I'll change a few words. When you hear a wrong word, raise your hand. If you remember what the right word was, say it aloud quietly.'* You may prefer to have your students make some audible signal such as tapping with their pencils, rather than a visible signal. What is essential here is that they make some muscular commitment of themselves; that they be aware of the times when others are noticing wrong words; and that a student need not feel punished or publicly embarrassed if he makes an error.

This step is a time-honored one and can build up a nice rhythmic interaction between you and the class. I have found that in order to make it go smoothly, I need to write in the margins or between the lines a good supply of suitably 'wrong' words. I can't think them up fast enough while I'm reading aloud.

If you use this step, you'll probably want to use it four or five times with a different set of 'errors' each time.

7. *'Now I'll read the text with pauses. During each pause, say that part of the text to yourself, or imagine you are saying it to someone else. Don't* repeat *it after me*: say *it!'* Here you are helping each student to bring the new composite of form and meaning to life within himself, rather than leaving it as a dead linguistic artifact to be copied mechanically.

8. *'This time I'll pause* before *each phrase. Try to think the words which follow before you hear them.'* Now at last the students are attempting silently the kind of production that memorization requires. Correct attempts receive immediate reward and so are strengthened. Incorrect attempts receive an immediate and nonpunishing correction.

9. *'Now listen once more to the entire text. Don't worry about the words. Just sit back and listen as though you were*

hearing it for the first time.' This is a good time for you to use an emphatic, almost triumphant tone of voice through which you imply without saying so, that the work of memorization has been successfully and happily completed. Leave perhaps 10 or 15 seconds of silence after the end of the text.

You may want to go on to a procedure which requires individual students to recite the text aloud or act it out in the conventional way. If you decide to do so, I'd suggest that you don't do it immediately. Let the text simmer on the back burner in the students' minds while you go on to some unrelated activity. You may even find it more efficient to wait until the following day before going on to production-based memory work.

7.3 Memorizing individual words

Like mimicry drill and the 'overlearning' of dialogs, the memorization of vocabulary lists is out of favor these days among many thoughtful and creative teachers. These teachers reason that genuine language is a two-sided combination of form and meaning, and that we should therefore minimize the occasions when students look at the form alone, or at form paired only with some more or less inexact equivalent in their own native language, and in lists rather than in context. Why not spend the time using the words in meaningful exchanges rather than shuffling a stack of flash cards?

In fact, I quite agree with this reasoning and put it into practice whenever I can. Nevertheless, I have found year after year that some students simply *will* make and use word lists. (I even catch myself at it from time to time in my own language study!) As we did with drills in general, it may be worth our while to take a second look at this primitive urge and at some of the ways in which it can be satisfied.

First let's dispose of a widespread but methodologically uninteresting reason for learning lists of words – the impending quiz 'over all the new words in chapters 2 and 3.' Such a quiz asks the student to 'give German translations for these English nouns,' or to 'choose the correct German equivalent for the following words.' About the most one can say for this sort of activity is that it enables a teacher with a minimum of work on his own part to check up on something measurable that is related to the students' knowledge of the language.

The real question is: why do some students insist on word-by-word vocabulary study even in a course where this kind of quiz is unknown? One reason is that some students bring with them a sense of moral obligation toward any word once it has come up. These people may become impatient with themselves when they can't think of a word, even if you as teacher put them under no pressure in this regard. They may even become annoyed with you if you *don't* give them a vocabulary test now and then.

But aside from any such moralistic motivation, a learner can see which of his word-images are defective at any given time, and which of these he is particularly interested in strengthening. He alone knows where those defects lie: in the second vowel, or in the final syllable, or in the native-language equivalent, or wherever. If he waited until these came up again in class or in printed materials, they would be unlikely to come up at the right time. So he needs a way to work on them when *he* is ready for them, and by himself. But working alone, it's hard to be very communicative. Frequently he ends up making himself an endless set of flash cards.

Most students know only one way to make and use flash cards: put the foreign word on the front and the native word on the back; then quiz yourself by looking at one side of the card and trying to give what's on the other, verifying or correcting your answers if necessary by looking at the second side; continue in this way until you can do the cards quickly and accurately.

Even with this simplest form of flash card, you may be able to point out to your students options that they hadn't thought of. One is the choice between reading the cards silently and reading them aloud. Many students, though perhaps not all, get more benefit from the latter. Another lies in what to do when one comes to a card to which one has given a wrong or incomplete answer. Some learners just put it on the bottom of the pack and continue through the rest of the stack in order. I have found it more helpful to stick the card back somewhere in the interior of the deck, anywhere from two to six cards from the top. That way I can build up the total image bit by bit without having to start from the beginning every time. Suppose, for example, that the native-language side of my card says 'air pollutants,' but that all I can remember of the foreign word is *luft..................ar*. I look at the other side and see *luftföroreningar*. If I merely read this word aloud and then put the card at the bottom of the stack, I may not do any better the next time it comes to the top. The new image containing the complete word may have faded too much. If, on the other hand, I put the troublesome card in the third position from the top, I can come to it while the image is fresher – perhaps even while it is still in short-term memory (chapter 4). This time I am able to supply more of the word: *luftför........ingar*. Looking at the other side of the card this time strengthens the neurochemical process (chapter 5) which produced the parts that were right, and at the same time supplies the corrections and other information that I still need. By the third or fourth try, I may be able to supply *luftföroreningar* intact, again receiving reinforcement when I check with the back of the card. Now I begin to place the card farther and farther back each time I meet it, until it is well beyond the range of short-term memory. Each time, I get the word back through a slightly different process, and so build up a little 'network of parallel pathways' of the kind that we talked about in chapters 4 and 5.

Using flash cards in this manner then becomes a process in which the learner observes his own learning, makes a series of simple but delicate choices, and lives with the results of his choices – something quite different from the dull mechanical routine which flash cards can be in the hands of some people.

If the language that you are teaching has nouns of different grammatical genders, you might suggest to your students that they write nouns of each gender in a distinctive color. The usual way to represent gender on flash cards is through articles (e.g. in German: *der Wein, die Stadt, das Ende*) or other words that agree with them, but these associations are still between words, and therefore presumably confined to the more verbal (for most people the left) hemisphere of the brain. The color gives to the other hemisphere something that it can hold onto, so that it can contribute also to the learner's picture of the word.

If your students make cards which are at least four or five centimeters from top to bottom, they also have choices open to them in how to use the space. The principle of the flash card is that each piece of information is located in its own area, which the user can look at without having to look at any other area. On a normal-sized flash card there are at least four such areas: the top and the bottom of the front and the back. If one of these areas contains the foreign word, a second may (for many words though perhaps not for all) contain the individual student's own drawing that represents for him something about the meaning of the word. The drawing may be representational or it may be

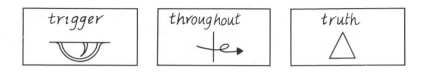

Figure 9

abstract, but its artistic quality and its intelligibility to anyone else are of course quite unimportant.

A third area may contain a short sentence or phrase with a blank where the word belongs: Don't pull the ....! several times .... the course. That's the whole .... If these phrases and sentences are taken from some connected and interesting reading that the student has been doing, they will reactivate relatively rich and well integrated images with a strong video component, thus bringing into play the less verbal side of the brain.

A fourth area may contain the native language translation of the foreign word. The student can easily work out a simple routine for producing the item in any one of these areas in response to the item in any other.

These, then, are a few of the options that you may help your students to explore in the memorization of vocabulary. Remember, though, that *none of them will lead to anything but learning* in the narrow sense in which we used that term in chapter 2. Depending on how much imagination the student puts into designing and using them, they may prove to be a relatively efficient precision instrument for getting selected items into long-term memory but they will do little or nothing toward transferring those items into permanent memory (chapter 4). If they are to have any lasting value, you (or the students, if they can manage it) must *take the items that are in LTM and use them in experiences that lead toward acquisition* (chapter 3). They can, however, be very useful in increasing the range of vocabulary that you have available to you in designing such experiences.

7.4 Learning paradigms

The third kind of material that language students may learn consists of paradigms: tables of the various forms of the same noun, adjective or verb arranged according to such grammatical characteristics as person, number, gender, tense or case. Here is a small sample of a verb paradigm in Portuguese:

	PRESENT TENSE	
	singular	*plural*
1st person	falar	falarmos
2nd person	falares	falardes
3rd person	falar	falarem

	PERFECT TENSE	
	singular	*plural*
1st person	ter falado	termos falado
2nd person	teres falado	terdes falado
3rd person	ter falado	terem falado

One common way of using a table like this is to convert it into a sequence and then learn to rattle off the items of that sequence in fixed order: *falar, falares, falar, falarmos, falardes, falarem* and so on. This has at least one serious disadvantage: your student may find himself out in the middle of a sentence and suddenly in need of the fourth item in the series, with no way to get it except to stop and run through the first three before he can retrieve the fourth. (This has happened to me often enough!)

Probably the other most common way of using a printed paradigm is to stare at it for a while (perhaps reading it aloud) and then trying to write it out. Some people always write the forms in the order given by the book, in which case this second technique is really not very different from the first. Others write the forms now in one order, now in another. This variation at least allows a bit of room for observing what one needs and making responsible choices accordingly. But it's hard to look back and check the accuracy of one form without inadvertently seeing some of the others, and this detracts from the self-testing, self-reinforcing feature.

For my own use as a learner, and for the use of some of my students, the best device I have found for learning paradigms makes use of cuisenaire rods. On an otherwise empty tabletop, lay out a replica of the paradigm. Perhaps the simplest is a single tense of a verb, with the one centimeter rods standing for first person, two centimeters for second person, and three centimeters for third person:

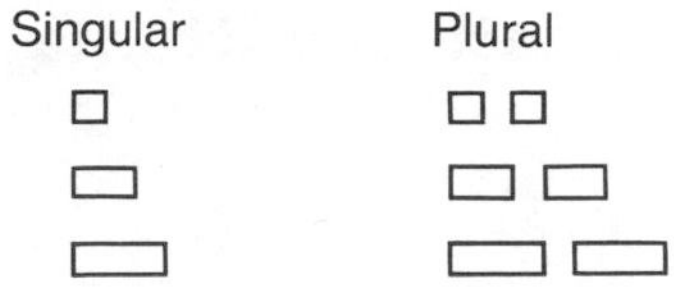

Singular   Plural

Figure 10

For more complicated paradigms, you can add your own conventions. This configuration contains the means for indicating *which* of the forms one is referring to, but without showing *how* the forms are spelled.

Two or more people work together in this technique, one (or more) in the role of learner, and one in the role of knower. The knower may be you the teacher, or a student with an open book. Either the learner or the knower points to the form which the learner is to try to produce. The learner then says the form aloud and the knower silently indicates whether it was right or wrong.

This technique has certain advantages. The silence of the knower, and the clear tabletop, minimize distractions and promote concentration. The colors and shapes of the rods themselves provide something for the less verbal side of the brain to relate to. The technique is very flexible and allows the learner to work extremely fast. Nevertheless, like flash cards and all of the other techniques in this chapter, *it leads only to learning* (chapter 3). At best, it helps students to sort out what they have met in earlier experiences with acquisition, or it makes a bit of new material more readily available for incorporation into future experiences. Your job as teacher is to keep track of this material and to guide the experiences.

8 Building grammatical patterns

8.1 Introduction

If you were to interview a hundred people on their feelings about the study of foreign languages, many of them would tell you they enjoyed it and many would tell you they hated or dreaded it. If you then asked the first of these groups exactly *what* they liked about learning languages, some might say they thought speaking was fun and others might talk of the pleasure of reading, but I doubt that many would pick the study of grammar. If you then turned to the second group and asked them what they *dis*liked most in languages, I suspect that grammar would be mentioned more frequently than anything else. Difficulties with grammar cause more discouragement and drive away more students than anything else in our profession. The teaching of grammar is for many new teachers the most formidable part of their undertaking. In this chapter and in chapters 9 and 10, I'll try to give you some basic ideas and a few widely usable techniques that may help you as you assume the most characteristic of a language teacher's responsibilities. First, the ideas.

8.2 Grammatical patterns – how we use them

Many theorists have pointed out the dual nature of language: how we use it to express meanings from the world outside language and also to shape and organize sound waves in the air or marks on paper. Every bit of language has some form and every bit of language has some meaning, and without both form and meaning our sounds and our scribbles are something else, not language.

In chapter 4, we drew a distinction between images and patterns. People figure out individual words and some sentences and their meanings in a language by comparing images and noticing that certain things in the linguistic component of those images seem to be tied to certain features of the nonlinguistic component. To take an extremely simple example, a child notices that among all the noises that he hears day in and day out, the sound 'doggie' comes up soon after the family dog enters his attention. Or he may notice that when he hears 'carrots' with a rising intonation he seems to have more options than he has when he hears the same word with a falling intonation.

In chapters 6 and 7, we looked at the learning of sounds and fixed sets of words – two kinds of *unit* at which we can arrive by a process of comparing images. But if we want to arrive at *patterns*, we have to compare *p* and *b* and *t* and *d* and discover that the *relationship* between (our composite image of) *p* and (our composite image of) *b* is the same as the *relationship* between (our composite image of) *t* and (our composite image of) *d*. (The difference, as we will see in chapter 18, is that the first member of each of these pairs is unvoiced and the second member is voiced.) Or we compare the relationship between *stay* and *stayed* with the relationship between *wait* and *waited* and find that they are the same; or we do the same thing with groups of sentences such as *He knew it; Did he know it? He threw it; Did he throw it?* To say that we have recognized a pattern is to say that we have found that a particular relationship between various sounds or words or sentences can be likened to relationships between other sounds or words or sentences.

Looking back at these last two paragraphs, I can see that they are perhaps more compact than anything that has come before them in this book. Perhaps a second, slow reading will make them clear. If that doesn't do the trick, I suggest that you ignore them and move on. The essential point that I was trying to make in those paragraphs was that patterns are one stage more abstract than words or sentences. Yet *without our ability to use patterns, we would be unable to understand or to produce any sentence that we had not heard before.* We would be little more than parrots.

For this reason it is extremely important that our students gain control of the patterns of the languages we are teaching them. There are really only four ways in which they can do so.

1. They can acquire them (chapter 3) much as a child acquires them out of the give-and-take of everyday communicative interaction.

2. They can meet them in activities which are in some sense communicative but which have been contrived by us to provide many examples of a particular pattern. We may even organize these activities so as to make it convenient for our students to notice the relationships.

3. They can focus very sharply on the relationships, in activities which do not require communication about matters outside the language.

4. For some patterns, there are fairly adequate short rules that they can learn. We frequently employ two or more of these four ways at the same time. Let's begin by looking briefly at the first.

8.3   Some techniques

Picking up grammar from ordinary conversation is an attractive idea, but I don't know of any method that relies solely on acquisition in its pure form for the imparting of structural control. The process would simply be too long and the outcome too uncertain. Every method has its own ways of organizing and trying to shorten it. Some begin by explaining each new point of grammar in the native language of the students, along with translated examples. This is certainly the quickest way to bring most people to some degree of intellectual understanding of the point, at least temporarily. Whether or not it is the quickest way to help them to internalize the point so that it will make a difference in how they speak or write outside of class is another matter.

At the opposite end of the spectrum stands the venerable Direct Method, so called because it doesn't present the foreign language through the medium of the student's native language. This is an example of the second way. If you follow this method, you present both the form *and the meaning* of each new point without making use of any language except the one you are teaching. On the most elementary level you point to objects and demonstrate actions. In a well-known example:

> I am closing the door.
> I am walking to the desk.
> I am picking up a book.
> I am opening the book.
>   and so on.

You can go on and show the differences between verb tenses by following the preceding series with:

    I closed the door.
    I walked to the desk.
    I picked up a book.
    I opened the book.
    and so on.

When you follow the Direct Method, you are using words and sentences not only to illustrate and practice how the language works, but also to manage the class and comment on what is happening. You are also putting acts and pictures in place of native-language equivalents. For all of these reasons, your students are taking in images which are relatively rich, diversified in sensory channels, and well integrated (chapters 3–5).

Once you have introduced a new grammatical contrast in this way, you can go on and summarize it in the form of a diagram or table, still without using the native language of your students. This is the third way of gaining control of the grammar of a foreign language.

I	*am*	clos	*ing*	the door.
I	*am*	walk	*ing*	to the desk.

I	clos	*ed*	the door.
I	walk	*ed*	to the desk.

Students can then go on to use the fourth way – they can learn the rules.

Because the Direct Method has been around for so many years, it has influenced most language teachers to one extent or another. Much creative imagination has been expended in finding tricks for putting across concepts without translation. I encourage you to borrow from the work of others, but also to make your own contributions to the mass of reusable experience. As you do, you will find that the discipline of working within the constraint of avoiding the learner's native language sharpens your perception of what you are doing. It is therefore excellent training for you, even if you don't plan to do most of your teaching that way.

Let us look at some more examples which show us how we can combine and choose between the different ways of working on grammar.

In general, as we will see more fully in chapter 9, a point of grammar is some kind of pattern in the target language: in

English the adjective *dependent* is generally followed by the preposition *on*. This pattern includes, either explicitly or implicitly, some contrast: the adjective *independent* is followed not by *on* but by *of* or *from*. Once the point of grammar is clear, students still need a certain amount of practice with it before it becomes a dependable part of what in chapter 2 we called their 'competence.' You can give them this practice in activities which simulate real-life use of the language, or you can give it to them in plain old grammar drills.

One notorious source of difficulty for students of English is choice of the right preposition – how to identify and respond to the signals that tell a native speaker which one to use. Thus a learner may say things like 'I live at London' or 'I am going in France.' You might work on this problem in the third way, perhaps with a nice, neat substitution–correlation drill (see p. 100). You might spend ten minutes on the drill on Monday, give it another five minutes on Wednesday and a final quick runthrough for three minutes on Friday, and then wonder on the following Monday why your students are still misusing the same prepositions in the same ways in their spontaneous speech.

In working on the same problem in the second way (p. 84), you may employ fictional but realistic material: a city map showing the homes of a list of imaginary people, or a portion of a mailing list for a fictional organization. You can quiz the students orally over this information, or you can have them work in small groups to put some of it into full sentences, complete with prepositions. (Compare what I have to say on pp. 100, 130 about this kind of work by small groups.)

You can do much the same thing with real information – the addresses of the people in the class, or the mailing list of a real organization. This can have obvious advantages in the forma- tion of images tied to fuller and deeper associations with things that really matter to your students. You will make the most of these advantages if you can avoid the body language and the tone of voice of a teacher working on grammar, and play the part of a human being who is vigorously interested in what you and your interlocutors are saying.

If you want to enrich the images still further, you can enlist not only the students' facts, but also their imaginations and their emotions. First, have each student write down the answers to two questions: 'Where in this city would you most like to live?' 'Where in this city would you *least* like to live?' Next, let them communicate their answers to one another in small groups.

(This shouldn't take much more than a minute.) Third, talk with individuals about their answers. In doing so, you can again create the atmosphere of brief but very real conversations. At the same time you can monitor the correctness of their replies, and by asking added questions of your own you can elicit replies with whichever prepositions you wish. Finally, ask 'Where did M say she would like to live?' 'Where would N not like to live?' These questions lead to additional practice, still in real conversation. They also require people to pay attention to one another and therefore leave individuals with the feeling that others have noticed what they said.

If you add 'and why?' after each of these two questions, the exercise will become both more interesting and more realistic. On the other hand, the practice with *in*, *on* and *at* will be less concentrated. This is one more of the many choices that are in your hands.

Another recurring difficulty for learners of English is in choosing between past and present perfect tenses: *was* versus *have been*. This also can be approached through a substitution –correlation drill:

	I was in England last year.
here	I was here last year.
since Tuesday	I've been here since Tuesday.
twice	I've been here twice.
a week ago	I was here a week ago.
	and so on.

As in the example with the prepositions, one can supply fictitious information and ask the students to put it into complete sentences:

Carl Summers	*Carol Winters*
Brussels 1972	Stockholm 1970–3
Paris 1973–4	Tokyo 1974
Amman 1975	Seattle 1975
Montevideo Jan. 1976	Djakarta 1976
Brussels 1977–8	Tokyo 1977
Ottawa since 1980	Honolulu 1978
	Tokyo since 1978

A sample product might include:
> Carl Summers was in Brussels in 1972. In fact, he's been there twice. He was there a second time from

1977 to 1978. He's spent three years there altogether. We don't think he's ever been to Tokyo, but we're not sure because we don't know where he was in 1979.

With regard to the students' long-term interests outside the classroom, this sort of thing may be trivial. Nevertheless it does require them to visualize the person and the itinerary and base their sentences on that meaning. They can no longer produce their sentences in the third way, listening to a cue, running it through some kind of pattern, and echoing it back.

Fictional information of this kind can be turned into simple games that provide some kind of goal which, though it is still a classroom artifact, goes beyond the mere production of sentences. Thus information about four individuals may have buried within it some principle which cannot be found by looking at what is known about any one of them: that each of the people has been in some one city twice, or that all of them were in some city at the same time, or that each of them moved consistently from east to west for example. The information about each fictional individual can be given to a different student in a group of four, or to a different small group in the class as a whole. You can find dozens of such ideas in books, and you can make them up yourself. My only purpose here is to give you a sample of what I meant on p. 84 by the 'second way' of working on grammar – practice which is contrived but still communicative, organized and interesting.

9 Building patterns through drills

9.1 Introduction

Now what about grammar drills? Many students expect them, many textbooks provide them, and the administration of your school may require you to use them. Yet you hear of highly competent teachers, some of them leaders in the profession, who get along without them and even avoid them. What conclusion should you draw?

The conclusion that you reach will be your own. In this chapter and chapter 10 I can only explore with you how grammar drills work, and show you how they fit in with some of the concepts that we talked about in earlier chapters. These include the concepts of 'learning,' security, short-term and long-term memory, patterns, images and (in chapter 8) the four ways of increasing one's control over the patterns of a language.

The second of those four ways was through communicative but organized – organized but in some sense communicative – use of the forms of the language. In a classroom activity which concentrates on the second of these ways, the images which the student is taking in are fairly well balanced between the form of the words and sentences, and the ideas which lie outside the words but which the words convey. Thus you may use objects or pictures which fit the meanings of what you are getting the students to say or understand, or you may discuss what they are interested in, or tell them an exciting story. For all of these, you carefully provide a good number of examples of the pattern in which you are interested.

In the third way of working on grammar, the student takes in images in which there is much less of a relationship between the linguistic meaning of the words and what is going on in the classroom at the time. Attention is frankly and fully focused on the pattern itself as a linguistic artifact, just as one might explore the operating characteristics of a clarinet by playing with and on it, or as one might try out a new dance step first in order to see how it works, and then to develop facility with it. When one is first engaging in either of these activities, one would just as soon not have a band playing in the background, or even a pianist tapping out music for one to follow. It is for reasons very much like these that many students can profit by some opportunity to work with patterns in the third way.

But to say that there is a time and place for the third way is one thing. To concentrate on this way to the virtual exclusion of the others is quite another thing. Unfortunately, something very much like that did happen during one period in the history of language teaching, with an understandably strong reaction against it on the part of many thoughtful teachers. My own view is that a new teacher can profit from seeing what grammar drills are and how they work, and how they and the other three ways of studying grammar can complement one another.

In this chapter and the next, then, let's look at a few of the types of drill that you are most likely to encounter in existing materials. This book is not the place for a complete, or even a lengthy catalog of all the kinds of drill that language teachers have devised over the centuries. And my emphasis in this chapter will be not on the drills themselves, but on what *you* can *do* with them.

9.2   The simple substitution drill

Perhaps the simplest grammatical drill of all is one in which the students substitute one short item after another in the framework of a single unvarying sentence. Here is an example:

	Where can I buy a leather wallet?
light bulb	Where can I buy a light bulb?
toothbrush	Where can I buy a toothbrush?
fountain pen	Where can I buy a fountain pen?
bicycle pump	Where can I buy a bicycle pump?

One thing to remember about this kind of drill is that it is supposed to be a systematic way of converting performance into competence. That is to say, the students are led to produce a series of phrases or sentences that have something in common, in the hope that as they do so they will develop some new inner resource that will enable them to produce phrases or sentences on the same pattern independently in the future. This may sound like hoping to charge the dry cells in a flashlight by placing the bulb in front of a strong light. The reason why this is not in fact a good comparison is that the human mind, unlike an electric circuit, can observe itself and shift its focus of attention. A student in producing the sentences of a drill for the first time may draw on some very general elementary competence such as the ability to repeat sounds after you, or the ability to read words off the page. As the drill proceeds, however, the student may notice or begin to feel the relationship which the drill was designed to illustrate, and may then begin to produce those same sentences on this new basis. If doing so leads to success, then (as we saw in chapters 4 and 5), the place of that observation in the student's mind becomes clearer and stronger, and more readily available the next time he needs it – to use the term that we used in those chapters, it is 'reinforced.' If you do the drill right, then you (1) draw on existing resources (competence) in your students to (2) produce new behavior (performance) which when rewarded by success (3) builds new resources (competence).

Your job is to take a drill like this and make it both interesting and useful to your students. This job will be easier if you are already prepared when you meet it. The only way to be prepared is to have in your mind – and in your muscles – a basic series of activities. In the next few pages I'll suggest one such series. It's not the only good series, of course, and you shouldn't expect to use every one of these activities with every drill. But having it at hand so that you can draw from it on the spur of the moment without needing to think about it can free your mind for more urgent matters. The familiarity of a routine will also free your students' minds and at the same time contribute towards their emotional tranquility. Here, then, are eight steps:

1. *You read the sentences of the drill aloud.* Let your students just listen. I generally ask people to keep their books closed during this step. Even if they don't understand all of the first sentence, they will understand parts of it. Since all of the sentences in a given drill are somehow related to one another, it follows that what they do understand from the first sentence will help them toward easier understanding of the second, and so on down the line.

I said that I usually have people keep their books shut as I read the sentences of a drill for the first time. You may decide that your class has such a need for security that you should let the books stay open. Here is one two-way choice in technique comparable to one of the choices that we made in chapter 6. As in the modeling of pronunciation, your delivery will be some combination of slow versus fast (a two-way choice), loud versus soft (another two-way choice), and playful versus plain versus emphatic in tone. The 12 combinations ($2 \times 2 \times 3$) of these choices are options that are available to you. These 12 options are, if anything, even more important here than in the modeling of pronunciation because now you want your students to respond to meaning as well as to sound. You now have $2 \times 12 = 24$ possibilities among which you can shift during this first step of the drill procedure that I am outlining. The practical effectiveness of this number is attested by one of my colleagues, who recalls that her best teacher of Turkish regularly used just such shifts as these with her. In this way he was able to keep a drill alive long after it would have died in the hands of most other teachers.

While you are busy with these choices, your students' task is quite different from yours. First of all, of course, they are trying simply to understand one sentence at a time. Beyond that, they are trying to go on from there and figure out what the principle or the purpose of that particular drill is supposed to be. This brings us to the second in my series of eight steps.

2. *Be sure that everyone sees how the drill is put together and what it's supposed to do.* This won't take much time. (If it does, then the drill probably isn't right for this class now!) Even so, you have a few very important choices available to you. The biggest is between stating the purpose of the drill yourself, or letting your students find it for themselves and state it in their own words. Stating it yourself will probably take a bit less time. That alternative may also be necessary if your class consists of people who very much want to put themselves into the hands of a capable and authoritarian teacher who will lead them clearly and firmly. On the other hand, what your students discover for themselves will be something that fits in with what they already know, something like a missing piece in a jigsaw puzzle. Your explanation, no matter how careful and simple, is unlikely to fit quite so well. In addition, their wording will be wording that they understand. So they are likely to remember it better, both in the later steps of this drill and beyond it. One way to start their thinking in a productive direction is to ask about the drill, 'What do these sentences have in common?'

There are advantages for you too when your students assume some of this responsibility. Listening to them, you can hear where their understanding is and how their minds are working.

You *won't* get this kind of information if you just ask them whether they've understood your statement about the drill and they answer 'yes.' In addition, your students may point out features of the drill which neither you nor the writer of the textbook had noticed.

Again you have the choice of what the students are to do with their books. You may ask them to leave them closed, or to have them open throughout this step, or to open them halfway through the step.

Referring to the drill on page 90, I thought that its principal purpose was to illustrate and practice the use of *can*. But it is also true that each sentence in that drill ends with a noun that is modified by another noun, and that the sentences also illustrate a simple question pattern with *where*. Finally, some textbook writers use drills of this type in order to introduce new vocabulary. If the students have already met the sentence *Where can I buy a leather wallet?* in some larger and more meaningful context, then other pairs of words can be substituted for *leather wallet*. The new words should of course be chosen for their relevance to the students' anticipated needs.

3. *Let your students listen to the drill again.* As far as technique is concerned, you have the same choices open to you that you had in step 1. The difference between that step and this one lies in what the students' minds are doing. In step 1, they were scrambling to understand the individual sentences and to begin to sort out what they were for. In step 2 that sorting-out process was completed. Now in step 3 the understanding from step 2 is proving its worth by the way in which it does indeed illuminate the sentences of the drill. During this step therefore, the students' minds have an opportunity to allow the integration of example with generalization, and of generalization with example, to begin.

In steps 1–3, except for quoting a few forms in step 2, your students have not yet had to remember or even to say anything in the language they are studying. The total elapsed time for these three steps is probably somewhere between one and three minutes.

4. *Have the students repeat the sentences of the drill after you.* The technique here is very much like the one for basic pronunciation practice (6.2) and, as in that procedure, you can switch from the full class to groups to individual students. You will probably want to vary the order of items and the order in which you call on people, again as in the pronunciation

procedure. This time, however, you are not concentrating on pronunciation, and so you correct it only if you hear something pretty far off. Your purpose now is to allow your students to form a fresh and clear image of these eight sentences – an image which will involve their own speech muscles as well as their ears and eyes. For that reason this fourth step may be relatively brief – perhaps a minute or so. Even though the step is brief, you will still have time to choose from among dozens of combinations of the same elements that you varied in the earlier steps.

There are several contrasting doctrines on just how this repetition step should be carried out. Some teachers believe that it should be done as loudly as possible and very fast, the students yielding themselves mentally and physically to the surging sound in which they are caught up. Insofar as this way works, it probably works precisely because of this surrender, which may shift the student's learning apparatus into some mode about which we know little. Other teachers prefer a pace that is more leisurely, but still steady, which allows the student time to notice what is going on and do a little conscious cognitive work on it. A third possibility is to leave a two or three second pause between your voicing of a sentence and the students' repetition of it. This allows even more opportunity for cognitive processing, while the auditory echo is still there for the students to fall back on if they need it.

As I have described this fourth step, it is only a preparation for the fifth step. Some teachers lengthen it, going through the sentences over and over, with the idea of 'working the pattern into the muscles.' I suspect that the greatest benefit from this style of drilling comes when students allow their minds to operate on successive repetitions in different ways. But I don't think anyone is sure on this point.

One thing I am fairly certain of: whatever physical energy is used in this step needs to be clearly and firmly channeled. I can see little value in strenuous exertion just for the sake of strenuous exertion; there is a vast difference between purposeful hubbub and irrelevant din.

5. *Have the students give you the complete sentences of the drill in response to cues that you provide.* This is the central step of the whole procedure. The cues or prompts in this particular type of drill may consist of the words that have been substituted for one another. For example, you give the first sentence (*Where can I buy a leather wallet?*) and then immediately say *light bulb.* A student designated by you then comes back with *Where can I*

buy a light bulb? You then go on to *toothbrush*, another student gives the next sentence, and so on through to the end of the drill. As an extra challenge you can give as cue only a single word or even just a single syllable. We will see in chapter 11 that some of the most effective cues are not words at all. Each kind of cue makes its own unique demands on the students, and so calls forth a slightly different kind of mental activity. Each cue with its response will become part of a new image, as I used that term in chapter 4. As you vary your cues, therefore, you help your students to form a richer set of associations *from and with* the experience of having gone through the drill with you.

When calling on students in random order, most teachers look or point at the student who is to reply at the time when they give the cue, or just before. Another option is to wait until a second or two after the cue and then call on someone. The purpose here, as in chapter 6, is to keep each student reacting at least silently to every cue, and not just to the ones that she knows will be directed to her.

How should you respond to an incorrect sentence from a student in a drill like this one? There's no one right answer to this question. In framing your own answers to it from day to day, you may want to keep in mind two principles, both of which we have already seen, and which will often pull you in opposite directions. One is the desirability of maintaining a steady rhythm of class activity (p. 52). The other is the importance of drawing the right answer, not merely out of the student's mind, but out of a part of her mind which will leave her with a small but lasting improvement in her own inner resources (pp. 13, 91).

It is commonplace among language teachers and some psychologists that animals (including the human ones) learn better if they are immediately rewarded for each correct response to the teacher's stimuli. It is also undeniable that a smile or a quick 'Very good!' from the teacher is in some sense a 'reward' for most students. *But there are two components to this reward!* The first and essential component is knowledge about the correctness of the response. The second is approval from you the teacher. This second component cuts both ways. For some students, the very giving of approval in this manner sets up and maintains a climate of evaluation which they dislike. Other students react in just the opposite way. They have a continuing desire for positive evaluation. But I have seen even these students react negatively to a string of 'Very good's' if they sense that what comes disguised as praise is really nothing more than a perfunctory way of trying to 'motivate' them.

It has seemed to me for several years now that the best way of reacting to a correct response is usually to say nothing at all, but simply to go on to the next cue. If your students understand this convention, the information they need will come across just as clearly as if you had said something. As for the second component – the emotional support – the same purpose is served when you maintain a steady rhythm in the activity *and seem to be enjoying it – and enjoying the students – yourself.* (You can't fool your students here, though. If you try to force an appearance of enjoyment, they will quickly spot it as counterfeit. Then the whole activity will become fatiguing both for you and for them. Genuine enjoyment, on the other hand, is contagious and restful.) And of course the non-overt reaction to a correct response simplifies the rhythm and saves time.

For many teachers the drill procedure stops here. I think, however, that there are at least two or three additional steps which you will often find useful. But even step 5 should not end here. In addition to whatever combination of techniques you use in this step, you need to have in mind the degree of mastery that you want your students to reach. Will you be satisfied when at least half of them can choke out the correct sentences in response to at least half your cues? Or will you continue the drill until 100 per cent of them can produce 100 per cent of the right answers with the ease and speed of native speakers? Your actual goal will no doubt lie somewhere between these extremes. If you have a pretty clear idea of just *where* it lies, both you and your students will find the drill more satisfying.

6. *Have individual students give single sentences that they remember from the drill.* This requires of the students a kind of mental activity which psychologists call 'immediate free recall.' This activity contrasts with what they were doing in step 5, where they were combining two echoes – one from the preceding sentence and one from your cue. I'm not sure exactly why free recall is so useful, but I would guess that there are at least two good things going on. One is that the students are now producing whole sentences without a cue. The other is that they have a chance to do so each in their own way. It's amazing how different people are from one another in how they approach a simple task like this one. In recalling the sentences, one will merely repeat aloud an auditory echo that's still reverberating, left over from step 5. Another will, in effect, read aloud from a

mental image of a printed sentence which she had formed from what she had heard (or, if her book was open during step 5, from what she had actually seen). I had something to say in chapter 4 and 5 about these differences. But students also differ in which sentences they choose to recall. Some will choose the safe way and give sentences that they are sure of. Others will seize the opportunity to try out something on which they want a bit more practice.

If you decide to use step 6, here are a couple of hints. First, have each student give only one sentence at a time. Otherwise the step may turn into a contest in which people who are not natural memorizers come out feeling inferior. (It's not a matter of general intelligence, but they may feel that it is. People differ much less in their ability to come up with some *one* out of eight sentences than in their ability to reproduce six or seven of the eight.) Second, repeat each sentence quietly and correctly as the students give them. This removes any uncertainty about whether any sentence was right or not, and removes any need for 'correcting mistakes' during this step. We are approaching the end of the drill, and it is time to emphasize confirmation, confidence and consolidation.

7. *Have the students reword the sentences.* They can do so in either or both of two ways: (a) By restating the same ideas in grammatically different form (e.g. *Where can light bulbs be bought?* or *Will you buy me a fountain pen?*) or (b) introducing other vocabulary into the same grammatical pattern (e.g. *Where can I buy a clay flowerpot?*) Here the students are taking greater responsibility for meanings. They also find in this step an opportunity to re-use other recently-learned words that they don't want to forget. Not least, they can now express their individuality, still within the framework of the drill and sup-ported by it, in ways that will interest or amuse their classmates and you.

8. *Talk with the students for a minute or two, using material from the drill.* In the drill that we have been using as an example, the most obvious way to do this would be to ask individual students whether they have, or where one can buy, a light bulb (etc.), or to have each one state which of the items in the list they would like to have as a gift. I'm afraid, though, that questions such as these would sound perfunctory, and so would fail to produce the desired effect. A more fruitful line of questioning might be something like: Can you use any of these items on its own? Which would be the most expensive? Which is

likely to last the longest? Which is probably the smallest? Would you buy more than one of any of the items? With just a minute or two of this sort of simple conversation, you can break up the artificiality of the drill situation, reminding your students and yourself that the real reason why people use a language is not to produce right answers, or even to increase their competence in it, but simply to say things to one another.

This is the end of the basic procedure that I have outlined for bringing one simple kind of drill off of the printed page. As I said at the beginning, you will seldom use all eight of these steps with any one drill. (The total amount of time spent on a drill probably shouldn't exceed five or ten minutes.) And you will undoubtedly find other steps that you will want to add to the ones that I have listed. The important thing is that you have your techniques – and their variations – at your fingertips before you begin to conduct the drill.

10 More about grammar drills

10.1 Introduction

Having discussed the simplest type of grammar drill in so much detail, we will be able in this chapter to deal more briefly with some other common ways of working directly on structural patterns. Before we go on to the other types of drill, however, it may be worthwhile to look at two processes that have been unfolding as we moved through this series of steps. The students' responses have required, and have come from, increasingly deep resources: the ability to understand individual sentences, the ability to see the relation among those sentences, the ability to echo complete sentences, the ability to echo and combine sentence and cue, the ability to recall whole sentences, and the ability to make original and appropriate modifications in known sentences. At the same time, you have stepped back from the center of the stage and taken a supporting role. The students' initiative is still within a clear framework that you have provided, but it is increasing steadily. As you navigate your way through the drill, you of course keep your eye on the book, for that is the map to your destination. You also keep your eye on the reactions of your students, for they are the airspeed indicator that tells you when the plane is in danger of stalling. But the contrast between minimum and maximum student initiative, and the contrast between superficial and deep sources for their responses — these are the cardinal points of your compass.

10.2 The substitution table

One widely used device is the substitution table. It is in effect a summary of a number of possible substitution drills derived from a single sentence. At the same time it provides a graphic representation of the surface structure of that sentence:

Where	can	I	buy	a	leather wallet?
	might	he	find	a	light bulb?
	will	she	get		
	did	I	sell		
	do	we			
	does				

You can do vigorous drills with a table like this in front of your class, concentrating on steps 4 and 5 of the basic procedure. Or you can have the students work in groups of two or three to see how many correct sentences they can write from it in some fixed period of time. The advantages of working in small groups are that students can check one another's work as they go along, and that in so doing they develop a valuable spirit of teamwork in competition with other groups. The table itself provides insurance against undetected errors, but if you think it necessary, you can provide a different kind of practice with the same material by having each group's work checked by another group.

10.3 The substitution–correlation drill

A second very common type of drill is very much like the simple substitution drill that we have already looked at. Again, a series of words or short phrases serve as cues for a series of sentences which illustrate some grammatical relationship. This time, however, the student doesn't merely insert the cue into a model sentence; he must also make some appropriate change in that sentence:

> You bought a leather wallet, didn't you?
> she   She bought a leather wallet, didn't she?
> they   They bought a leather wallet, didn't they?
>   and so on.

This drill is built around a problem that plagues learners of English regardless of their native language: the fact that English has a whole set of non-interchangeable counterparts for French *n'est-ce pas?* Spanish *¿no es verdad?* German *nicht wahr?* Turkish *değil mi?* and so on.

The same basic sentence can serve for more than one such drill:

<table>
<tr><td></td><td>You bought a leather wallet, didn't you?</td></tr>
<tr><td>will buy</td><td>You will buy a leather wallet, won't you?</td></tr>
<tr><td>are buying</td><td>You are buying a leather wallet, aren't you?</td></tr>
<tr><td></td><td>and so on.</td></tr>
</table>

Each of these drills requires the change to be made in some one slot in the sentence. Two single-slot drills are often combined to make a multi-slot substitution–correlation drill:

<table>
<tr><td></td><td>You bought a leather wallet, didn't you?</td></tr>
<tr><td>she</td><td>She bought a leather wallet, didn't she?</td></tr>
<tr><td>is buying</td><td>She is buying a leather wallet, isn't she?</td></tr>
<tr><td>they</td><td>They are buying a leather wallet, aren't they?</td></tr>
<tr><td>will buy</td><td>They will buy a leather wallet, won't they?</td></tr>
<tr><td></td><td>and so on.</td></tr>
</table>

The same basic steps that I have outlined for the simple substitution drill will work, with a few small and obvious modifications, for this type of drill as well.

10.4 The transformation drill

A third type of drill also requires the students to produce sentences in response to cues, but this time the cues are whole sentences. The simplest drills of this type are the familiar 'Change this sentence to the negative,' or 'Change these sentences to the past tense.' Other transformation drills illuminate for students some of the less elementary points of the language:

> I bought the wallet from a salesman.
>> Which salesman did you buy the wallet from?
> I bought the light bulb from a store.
>> Which store did you buy the light bulb from?
> I bought the toothbrush from a drugstore.
>> Which drugstore did you buy the toothbrush from?
>> and so on.

The basic procedures for this drill are again the same as for the simple substitution drill (9.2). This time, however, the length of the cue will change the rhythm of activity and slow things down a bit. One way to compensate for this effect is to modify the tone in which you give the cue, dramatizing slightly your own thoughtfulness about the cue and your interest in what the student is going to say in response.

Notice that each of the two columns of sentences in this drill could serve as the responses in a substitution drill. For example:

	I bought the wallet from a salesman.
fountain pen	I bought the fountain pen from a salesman.
store	I bought the fountain pen from a store.
light bulb	I bought the light bulb from a store.
	and so on.

Transformation drills may be combined with one another and with one-word cues for some purposes. Speakers of most other languages find that it's hard to get used to prepositions and certain adverbs at the end of a sentence, either to put them there themselves or to understand them when native speakers put them there. The following sequence can help them to develop a feel for this feature of colloquial English:

record   Do you see that record over there?

He wrapped that record over there up in some expensive paper.

This is the expensive paper that he wrapped that record over there up in.

She threw the expensive paper that he wrapped that record over there up in away.

What did she throw the expensive paper that he wrapped that record over there up in away for?

book   Do you see that book over there?

He wrapped that book over there up in some expensive paper.

This is the expensive paper that he wrapped that book over there up in.

She threw the expensive paper that he wrapped that book over there up in away.

What did she throw the expensive paper that he wrapped that book over there up in away for?

and so on.

From your student's point of view, each line of this drill consists of a variable part (record, book, etc.) and an invariable part (Do you see that .... over there? He wrapped that .... over there up in some expensive paper, etc.). Getting the whole sentence right requires the student to give attention to each of these two parts. But the *kind* of attention that is required is quite different from one part to the other. It is one thing to remember which of a list of short words you're supposed to be using at any given moment. It is another thing entirely to reproduce a string of words, especially when the structure that holds them together is something that you're still struggling to assimilate. For some reason, alternating between these two kinds of attention seems to increase the effectiveness of the practice rather than diluting it.

This last example that I have given contains sentences that are so long and complex that they become as much puzzles as drills. Even native speakers who would use and understand such sentences orally in context might hesitate a bit in reading or writing them. Many teachers would avoid them altogether, and I certainly hope no-one tries to turn them into booming choral repetition. But as a means of walking through a common English structural pattern and exploring it on the way, such extreme forms of drill still may have their place.

You don't have to get all of your drills out of published textbooks, of course. Whatever method you are following, you may decide from time to time that your students would profit from the chance to examine the structure of a particular sentence and get the feel of some pattern which that sentence exemplifies. That will be the time for you to create your own drills. When you do, here are four steps that you might think about:

1. Write out the sentence just for yourself. If the sentence is long, simplify it in a way that preserves the point you are interested in. For example, suppose that you'd like to familiarize your students with the way the *-ing* form of the verb is used in the sentence 'His voice rasping from a cold and his schedule distorted by the long session, B........ did not attempt to hide his irritation at D........'s tactics.' You might shorten this to 'His voice rasping, he answered angrily.'

2. Supply between three and seven more sentences that follow the same pattern. If the sentences are almost identical in vocabulary, you may turn them into a substitution drill:

> His voice booming, he answered angrily.
> His voice crackling, he answered angrily.
> His voice breaking, he answered angrily.
> and so on.

If they vary greatly in vocabulary, you will have to turn them into a transformation drill:

> His voice rasped, and he answered angrily.
> His voice rasping, he answered angrily.
> His face reddened, and he apologized.
> His face reddening, he apologized.
> and so on.

3. Be sure that the point you are teaching is included in the response sentences of your drill.

4. If you are going to make individual copies for your students, be sure that cues and responses are arranged on the page in such a way that the students can see each cue without at the same time inadvertently catching a glimpse of the response. In this way if they use the page for independent study, they will be able to test themselves by looking at the cues one at a time, and verify their responses by uncovering the full sentences as they need them.

There are two other common types of drill which you can make up readily as you need them. One gives a series of lexically unrelated sentences with blanks in them and directs the student to fill in the correct form of the verb in brackets at the left of the sentence, or the correct preposition from a list given at the head of the drill, or something of the sort. The other consists of sentences without blanks, into which the student is supposed to insert some specified word (*not, already,* etc.) in the proper place. Many students automatically write words in the blanks in their books. If you can persuade them to do their writing on a separate piece of paper, they will get more practice at the time. In addition, the book or duplicated sheet will continue to be usable for further oral practice when they want to review it a few days or weeks later.

10.5 Conclusion

Chapters 8, 9 and 10 have been about ways of helping people to gain better and better control of the grammar of a new language. I say 'gain better and better' rather than 'achieve' because the changing of one's competence in this area is a gradual one and I don't want you to become discouraged if a point that you were sure you had 'put across' one day seems to have been forgotten the next. The very idea of 'putting' a point 'across' fails to take account of the patience that you need in matters of this kind. I say 'helping people to' rather than 'causing people to' because many points of grammar are actually unnecessary for someone who wants only to be understood: 'Me come yesterday you no here' gets its message across about as effectively as 'I came yesterday but you weren't here.' The correct forms are therefore optional refinements, and anyone who holds onto these refinements does so for her own reasons.

Teaching them is thus something like painting a house. If the wood is clean and dry – if it is receptive – the paint will stick to it and last for many years. If the surface is not ready, the paint will blister and peel and soon be gone. The atmosphere in the classroom and the kind of person you are can influence your students' developing attitudes toward the language and its speakers, and thus provide a more receptive surface for the techniques in these three chapters.

11 Audiovisual and other aids

11.1 Introduction

Words and words, and words about words! That's what your classwork can become if you use nothing but a book. In chapters 3–5, we talked about the total memory-images that your students will store along with the vocabulary and grammar that you and the textbook expose them to. It's true that words used skillfully can bring themselves to life – an interesting conversation, a story that really fires people's imaginations, and so forth. This chapter, however, is about some of the means that you can use in order to provide direct sensory enrichment to the images that your students will take away with them.

11.2 Visual aids

The best-known sensory aids are visual. Before I begin to list some of their uses, let me make one general point that teachers sometimes overlook: *the background* against which you set the aid *can be as important as the aid itself*. The background both contrasts with the aid and supports it. With visual aids, the contrast may be in color or in texture. More important than contrast is support. The background should be a surface or an area which on its own merits does not repel the students' gaze. Otherwise the aid will receive a minimum of attention, and the 'peripheral stimuli' that are stored in memory along with the aid itself will be less helpful than they might be. *A corollary: in general the sensory background should be reassuring, therefore uncluttered, therefore simple.*

Traditionally the most frequent use of visual aids has been simply to illustrate what words are saying. Thus, you bring to class a cup, a saucer, a knife, a fork and a spoon and teach the class to say 'That is a teacup' or 'Where is the fork?' or 'Is the spoon to the right of the saucer, or to the left of it?' This is certainly a legitimate use of these objects, but there are at least a half dozen other uses of visual aids, a few of which teachers sometimes overlook. Let me just list them for you.

A second well-known use for visual aids is to provide cues in some simple types of drill. Suppose for example that your students have been saying 'How much costs that?' You want to give them an opportunity to focus their attention for a few moments on the correct form. One way to do so is to lead them through a simple substitution frame. You may bring to class a number of items that your students might want to buy, and have them repeat after you sentences like:

How much does that wallet cost?
How much does that book cost?
How much does that camera cost?
etc.

Then (as in chapter 9) you say 'How much does that wallet cost? Book.' A student replies with 'How much does that book cost?' In using visual aids as cues, you hold up the book or point to it instead of saying the word.

You can also use visual aids in order to elicit nonverbal reactions from your students: 'Point to the teaspoon.' 'Put the saucer on top of the cup and the spoon on top of the saucer.' 'Now put things into their proper places.' 'Set all of the objects in a single line according to their weight.' In addition to contributing a sensory element to the students' experience with the words, this technique has the advantage of allowing them to participate in the use of language without having to produce it themselves. In this way you will be able to expose them to new words and constructions without reducing their feelings of security. As they listen and respond they are building in their minds the competence that will make production possible a day or two later.

Up to this point, the only visual aids I've mentioned have been three-dimensional objects. Pictures can serve most of the same purposes as objects. They have the obvious advantage of being easier to carry around. In addition, you can find pictures of some things that simply aren't available in the classroom either for physical reasons (a sunset, a busy streetcorner) or for financial reasons (an expensive wristwatch). Pictures also vary greatly in complexity all the way from an apple, a bicycle or an article of clothing to a scene depicting in detail an incident involving several people.

You can use even the simplest picture (or object) for a number of purposes: naming the object of course, but on other occasions you may want to talk about color, size, function or value, or about your students' aesthetic or emotional reactions to it.

The more complex pictures are even more versatile in this respect. I once collected a set of interesting pictures and mounted each in its own folder. Opposite it I placed two or three sheets of paper with alternative exercises or stories about that same picture. My students were able to borrow these folders the way one borrows a book from the library, and use each story or activity in any way that they felt ready for. Here is a sample set of parallel written materials for one picture. (Notice that in the elementary section the answer to the first question is a device for introducing the people in the picture, and that this information is necessary for replying to the second and third questions.) Depending on their level of mastery and degree of adventurousness, different students found in these materials (1) practice with a new combination of familiar vocabulary and grammar, or (2) opportunities to figure out from the verbal and pictorial context the meanings of unfamiliar words and expressions, or (3) in a few cases, a meaningful text to copy in their own handwriting. (A number of people have reported to me that they find the physical act of writing to be a great aid to memory in foreign language study.)

Elementary level

What are these boys' names?

　　Their names are Paul and David Stark. The older one
　　is Paul and the younger one is David.

What is Paul wearing?

　　He is wearing a coat and a shirt.

What is David wearing?

　　He is wearing a pair of trousers and a shirt.

What is Mrs Stark wearing?

　　She is wearing an apron and a dress.

What kind of shirts are the boys wearing?

　　They are wearing sport shirts.

What kind of shoes is Mrs Stark wearing?

　　She is wearing black high-heeled shoes.

What kind of shoe is on the closet floor?

　　It's a tennis shoe.

What is that on the closet door?

　　It's a garment bag.

What kind of ball is that on the closet floor?

It's a baseball.
What is that beside the baseball?
It's a baseball bat.

Intermediate level

Small boys don't wear suits very often. They never stop growing, though. So if you buy a suit for a boy who is eight or ten years old, you can't be sure how often he will use it.

The Stark family is going to a wedding this afternoon. Mrs Stark has already put on a good dress and her best shoes. Now she is trying to get Paul and David ready.

Mrs Stark: Boys, put your good clothes on. We have to leave the house in twenty minutes.

Paul: What shall *I* wear?

Mrs Stark: Your blue suit, of course.

Paul: But my blue suit isn't comfortable, and I haven't worn it since last winter. My other clothes are *much* more comfortable!

Mrs Stark: Yes, but at a wedding everyone is supposed to dress up. You've grown a lot since winter, but I think you can still wear your suit.

Paul: The trousers fit me, but the coat's too small. What shall I do?

Mrs Stark: Take the suit off. Maybe David can wear it. He's grown a lot since winter, too.

David: The coat fits, but the trousers are too long for me. Paul's belt's too big for me, too.

Mrs Stark: Yes, the trousers *are* too long, and the belt *is* too big. You've grown a lot since winter, but you haven't grown enough yet. You'll be big enough for Paul's suit next spring, but what shall we do in the meantime? I'm afraid you'll have to wear your regular school clothes today.

Paul and David: Oh, boy!

Advanced level
(colloquial American English with few restrictions on grammar or vocabulary)

Everybody has problems. But it seems as if people with growing boys have more problems than anybody. At least, they have *different* problems. Take for example Mrs Sargent.[1] She has two boys – Billy, who is eight, and Walt, who has just turned six. The boys get along together fine, but they are so active that their mother has a hard time keeping their clothes clean and mended. Mrs Sargent has taught them, though, that their best clothes are not meant to be played in; the blue suit that she bought for Billy a year and a half ago is still in pretty good shape.

Last Saturday the family went to a wedding so Mrs Sargent got out Billy's suit and tried it on him. Billy moved his arms back and forth a little and then said 'Mother, the coat is too tight for me. It's a lot tighter than it was last winter. The sleeves aren't long enough. The trousers are all right, though.'

His mother sighed, but she had to agree with him. 'Yes,' she said, 'I'm afraid you've grown since January. You're just too big for this suit. Maybe Walt can wear it.'

About this time, her husband came in, so she asked him, 'Dick, do you think Walt can wear Billy's blue suit? It's much too good to throw away.'

Mr Sargent, who is an artist, squinted at the suit and squinted at Walt; and then he said, 'I'm afraid Walt hasn't grown quite enough yet. But you can try it on him.'

She tried the trousers on him, but they were much too long. Mrs Sargent said, 'Well, they'll have to wear their regular school clothes today and we'll just have to get two new suits. That's all there is too it.'

Her husband moaned. 'Where are we going to get enough money to pay for them?' was all he could say.

But they did. Can you guess where he got enough money for two new suits?

So far, I've mentioned just three uses for an object or a picture: to illustrate a word, sentence or story, to call forth specific verbal responses, and to produce nonverbal responses to them. A fourth use is as a non-specific stimulus for conversation or for writing. A simple example would be a loaf of bread, with a request that members of the class (or of small groups within the class) tell something of an early memory concerning bread. Or

---

[1] Sargent is the name of the artist who painted the cover. His legible signature appears in the lower right-hand corner of the picture.

you might show the class a complex picture for just 30 seconds or a minute and have the members of small groups pool their recollections of it. Finally, let spokespersons for the groups compare results. Or display an attractive travel poster and ask, 'If you were free to walk about in this area, where would you go first, and why?' Replies can be oral or written.

Fifth, you can use pictures in combination with other media not as illustrations but as sources of information that is unavailable elsewhere. As a simple example, you tape-record a conversation in which two or three speakers are discussing four people who are about the age of your students. Accompanying the tape are pictures of the four without their names. The recorded conversation contains some physical description of each one, but also numerous facts about their personalities and their abilities. A preliminary task for students would be to match pictures with names. A second task would be to answer the question, 'Which of these would you rather have sit next to you for three hours on a plane or train, and why?' Some of the reasons might come from the pictures and others from the tape.

Similarly a schedule for an airline can become the key to answers to questions about conversations which the students 'overhear' on a tape. The question is, 'Which flight did/will these people take?' One such conversation might include:

'Oh, I hope we're not late!' 'Don't worry. If we miss this one there's another in 45 minutes.'

The crucial lines in another might be:

'Have you eaten today?' 'No, I thought we were going to get breakfast on the plane, but we didn't.'

A sixth and very common use for pictures and objects is as background for everything else that goes on in the classroom: depending on the language, a travel poster of a French vineyard, for example, or a colorful Mexican *serape*, or a large menu from an Italian restaurant, or an attractive Japanese tea set. Choose such items not only for how they will brighten up the room. Take into account also their sensual appeal – the immediate rewards that they will give to anyone who looks at them or touches them. Take into account also the scope that they allow for the students' imagination. Not least, give some thought to what each of these 'mere decorations' *implies* about the country that it came from.

A seventh power of visual aids is to concentrate the attention of students for a period of time. I gave some examples in chapter 7. Just remember that 'concentrating' attention is something quite different from 'attracting' it. The best means for this purpose is a visually simple figure which moves slowly or is stationary against a visually simple background. (Don't overlook yourself and your clothing as visual aids, either!) Of course you will never use a visual aid solely in order to concentrate attention – you will always have some other end in mind at the same time. But when you have a choice between two pictures or two objects in pursuing that end, take the one that will make concentration easier.

These, then, are some of the main reasons for using visual aids. In presenting visual aids you may make use of a number of mechanical devices. Let me say just a word about three of them. They are the flannelgraph, the overhead projector and the filmstrip or slide projector.

The flannelgraph

Have you ever noticed that two pieces of flannel will stick to each other if you press them together, even when you hold them in a vertical position? The flannelgraph, which takes advantage of this principle, is a visual aid that is both inexpensive and surprisingly flexible. Cover a large board with flannel and draw on it an outdoor scene, a street, or some other large picture. Then on smaller pieces of flannel draw or paste smaller pictures – of people, animals, or movable objects. You can now make these smaller pictures take appropriate places in the larger scene and move them around to illustrate various sentences or to follow the progress of a story.

The overhead projector

This device allows you to take any book or paper and project it onto a wall or screen. There are great advantages in being able to do so when you are trying to use small pictures with large classes. You may also want to project a page or drawing from a book. The advantage of this is that students all focus on one image without distractions. Or perhaps you will want to project a student's paper on the screen and discuss with the class some of the ways in which the paper could be improved. In order to spare embarrassment to individual students and at the same time make the lesson of first-hand interest to more than a single student at a time, you might try this: Type out a paragraph which contains mistakes gleaned from several papers. If your class is not too large, you may be able to include at least one mistake from everyone's paper. Let the students pick the mistakes out and then correct them. Every time a mistake is found or corrected, you can mark it on the transparency.

The film strip or slide projector

These can be used to bring alive the customs, the people or the landscape of the country whose language is being studied. Film strips and slides can also nowadays be used in conjunction with a book and cassette. (I will discuss this use in 11.4.)

11.3 Audio aids

The least used and least understood of all audio aids is structured silence. By this term I mean silence of two seconds or two minutes in duration which is one part of some regular procedure or which the teacher announces in advance. All teachers are aware of the danger in *awkward* silence – in silence which the students sense that the teacher did not plan. Awkward silence is a rapid way to destroy your students' feelings of security with you as their teacher. Perhaps it is for this reason that some teachers go to great lengths to avoid silences of either kind.

Yet *structured* silence makes possible a feature that we can get from nothing else. The only science experiment that I remember from my early school years was one in which we were told to put a few centimeters of soil in the bottom of a jar, then fill the jar with water and shake it. After we stopped shaking it, the soil began to settle so that we could see through the water. The next morning we discovered that the random particles of ordinary soil had organized themselves into a neat sedimentary pattern and the liquid itself was clear.

In any class no matter how well planned, and for almost any student no matter how clear headed, the ongoing events of teaching and reciting are like a continual gentle (or not so gentle!) shaking of that jar. Only an occasional structured silence can give him a chance to get his own bearings and begin to sort things out for himself without distractions from you or from his fellow students. You can use a relatively long period of silence either at the end of the hour, or after a major explanation of grammar, or after a story or a poem. You can also use very short silences before and after each in a series of activities just to set them off from one another. At certain stages in drilling or in question-and-answer practice, some teachers have their students wait a few seconds before speaking. They find that this improves accuracy. If you allow students to pause before telling about something that comes either out of their memory or out of their imagination, you may find that they are working with more fully formed ideas, so that the language practice is more meaningful for them. And silence concurrent with the use of some visual aids can dramatically enhance their impact.

The tape recorder

For over 30 years now the portable tape recorder has been by far the most widely used of all audio aids. Let me just list seven of its functions.

1. Historically the oldest use of the tape recorder is as a replacement for the phonograph. In this capacity it provides the students with an audible replica of something in the textbook: it takes words off the page and lets students hear how they sound in the mouths of native speakers. Elementary as this use may seem, don't disregard it.

2. Tape recording makes it possible for students to record and listen to their voices economically and with a minimum of delay. When this new equipment first came into our hands, we thought it would work wonders. As soon as students heard themselves, we reasoned, they would hear and overcome many of their errors.

3. This reasoning was even more convincing with the coming of double-track recording. Under this system the teacher's voice was recorded on one of two parallel tracks, leaving pauses for the student's voice. The student could hear this track but could not erase it or record on it. His own voice, as he repeated after the master track, went onto the second track. Having listened and repeated, he could then rewind the tape, throw a switch, and listen to both tracks together. This surely must have been the magic road to excellent pronunciation!

For some students we were right. For many others, their first experience of this kind was salutary because it shattered a false complacency about how good they sounded. After a few such episodes, however, their ears became numb to the discrepancies between the teacher's voice and their own. In any case, once an individual student's self-critical faculties had been sharpened as much (or as little) as they could be by this device, the rewinding and listening process began to consume more time than it was worth.

4. The tape recorder can provide information which is not in the textbook but which is an essential part of the lesson plan. After your students have listened to a paragraph or an anecdote, for example, you can have them:
— answer printed questions about it; or
— fill in words which have been omitted from a printed transcript; or
— copy it off the tape; or
— write it in their own words; or
— talk or write about their own reactions to it; or
— use information from the tape in order to solve a puzzle or draw a picture.
You may be able to think of other possibilities.

5. The tape may provide not words but sounds: a single drop of water splashing into a full cup, a car stopping suddenly, a squeaking hinge, etc. Students can then talk or write, either individually or in groups, about the pictures which one of these sounds or sequences of sounds has brought to their minds.

6. You can play music typical of the country or countries where the language is spoken. This can be for relaxation and enjoyment only. Or the experience of listening can become the basis for a brief lecture by you, or for discussion of the students' reactions and their preferences.

7. Music that precedes an activity or accompanies it can greatly increase the effectiveness of the activity. What is essential in this use of music is not its cultural authenticity. It is rather the physical rhythm of the music, and the mood which it creates.

Making your own tapes

If your language is one of the widely taught ones, you can find professionally produced tapes for any of these seven purposes, many of which are expertly done and of top quality both pedagogically and acoustically. But by the very fact that they come from faraway experts, they can never fit your class exactly. For this reason you may want to make your own tapes from time to time. For example, you may take the content of a class discussion, summarize it in a two or three minute recording, and use it as in 4, above. Making your own tapes is cheap and quick. If you are new at it, though, you may want to keep in mind certain points about timing and also about the mechanics of recording.

Nothing will bother a student's ear and tire his body like unwanted noise. Fortunately there are a few tricks for reducing it even if you're using an inexpensive portable recorder. First of all, keep the microphone close to your mouth. (Don't put it directly in front, however, or some of the consonants will come out as unpleasant pops or rustlings!) If you are holding the microphone in your hand, be careful not to rub or tap it as you speak. If the microphone is built into the machine, the recorder will pick up its own mechanical noise. You can reduce this by setting the apparatus on a cushion. If the room is plastered, you can cut down the echo by hanging coats and blankets on racks and walls.

With regard to timing, the best advice for a speaker inexperienced at making tape recordings is usually 'Slow down!' This of course does not mean that you should distort your words by dragging them out unnaturally. It does mean that you must for most purposes avoid the rapid and relaxed articulation that you would use with a friend who was standing next to you. Perhaps the safest compromise is to imagine that you are speaking thoughtfully to three native speakers who are seated in different parts of a good-sized room.

In timing pauses for student repetition, mouth each sentence silently immediately after you have spoken it. (Don't just *think* the sentence. Actually make your lips move!) Then mouth the words 'One, two.' Then go on to the next sentence. In this way you will allow enough time for your students, who are not as nimble as you are at pronouncing your language.

The language laboratory

For some students with 'a good ear' the language laboratory is a marvellous opportunity to hear the faults in their own pronunciation and correct them from the model. Other students may simply become used to hearing the discrepancies between their own voice and the teacher's voice, so progress may be slow but even for these students the language laboratory is useful. The main advantage of the laboratory is of course that each student can work at his own speed and the teacher can 'tune in' without the student knowing and feeling nervous.

11.4 Audiovisual combinations

One device on the market combines a tape recorder and an automatic slide projector. You can select your own series of slides and write a bit of commentary or exercise material to go with each one of them. You then record this material on the machine. As you come to the end of what goes with one slide, you press a button. This button places an inaudible tone on the tape. As the tape is played back, this tone will cause the slide projector to move to the next picture.

The possibilities for this device are endless and to me quite exciting. You can make alternative sound tracks for a single set of slides, varied according to the students' proficiency, or according to any of several purposes: listening, practicing a recurrent structural pattern, answering questions, and so on. Not least, the equipment is relatively compact and portable, and costs a small fraction of the price of a videotape playback machine. It is useful either in class or in the laboratory.

As I mentioned earlier, some published courses have accompanying slides and filmstrips. As well as being used with cassettes, these can be used to pre-teach vocabulary and/or language points, to set the situation, as a stimulus for follow-up activities such as a role-playing or written work, or as a review. Videotape is also becoming increasingly popular although it is obviously expensive.

11.5 Other sensory aids

Sight and hearing are the only senses that can serve as channels for *language*, but they are by no means the only channels for *experience*. Tasting, smelling, touching and moving are constant sources of sensory data even when we fail to notice them. They can provide important background for the linguistic experiences on which by custom we are used to focusing attention. Sharing experiences of taste or smell or touch or motion can bring a group of people closer to each other. And of course these experiences are excellent sources of something to talk or write about. Folk dancing, wine tasting, or (an old standby of language teachers) a bagful of objects to be examined only by the fingers and then described – these are some simple applications of this principle.

11.6   Conclusion

There's a lot more to be said about the equipment that's available these days for audiovisual enhancement of a language curriculum, but I'm not in a position to say it. For reasons that are mostly budgetary, I've had only a little firsthand contact with videotape or with some of the more sophisticated language lab designs. What contact I've had makes me sure of two things: (1) If you have them available, they can be endlessly useful. (2) They can be useful only to the extent that both you and your students know exactly what you want them to do for you. Students who are sent to the lab just to 'listen to tapes' will tend to fall asleep or twist the headset cord or do homework for other courses. They're less likely to fall into these practices if they have a verifiable task, whether that task is memorizing, mastering some aspect of pronunciation, retrieving information or something else. As always, the machine is only as good as the people who control it.

12 Ways to oral activity: the teacher's questions

12.1 Introduction

When I was about 11 years old, my brother and I tried our hands at making model airplanes. They were the kind that consist of balsa wood and tissue paper and lots and lots of glue. All I remember about mine is that it was a biplane, and blue, and that it never got into the air. My brother's flew fine. I twisted the propeller in mine until the rubber band was tight and set the plane down at the end of the driveway, but nothing happened except that the propeller flapped around a few times until the rubber band ran down again. Maybe I used too much glue. I'll never know.

I think about those two planes sometimes when I watch learners and teachers of languages trying to engage in 'free conversation' or some other 'communicative activity.' Some conversations soar like birds, and some just sit like Mark Twain's 'Celebrated Jumping Frog of Calaveras County' – or like my old blue biplane. Maybe my lack of success with the plane should prevent me from using it to make points about language teaching, but I do think it provides a good analogy for understanding a few of the reasons why our best-planned teaching devices sometimes flop – or fly.

One of the conditions for flight (I am told) is that the plane should have a good amount of wing surface on each side. A huge right wing and a tiny left wing, or a huge left wing and a tiny right wing, simply will not do. In the same way there are always two sides to any use that we make of language: content and form, or what we say and the words, sounds and grammar that we need in order to say it. At times students have something that they desperately want to say, but lack the wherewithal to say it. At other times they sit there with a whole lapful of new words and grammar rules that you want them to practice, but with nothing special to say. Your job here is not to supply an entire wing, and certainly not both wings. It is rather to see where the imbalance lies and to supply what is missing. Putting things in this way is a bit abstract and metaphorical, of course, but I think that in the pages that follow you will see what I mean.

The model airplane illustrates one other point which should be obvious but which we sometimes forget: outside of the language classroom people never talk unless they have a reason to. That reason may be to ask for the salt, or to sell a bicycle, or to act polite, or simply to be sociable, but it is never to 'practice the present perfect tense.' To ask them to do the latter is like picking up the model plane and tossing it through the air: without its own power – even if its wings are large and well-balanced – it will very soon crash.

12.2 Oral activity in the classroom: its content

In chapters 8–10 we looked at several ways of constructing or repairing the right wing of the plane – the linguistic structures. Here we will concentrate on what the left wing – the content – is made of, and on ways of balancing one wing against the other. First a few characteristics of the content – of what you expect/ask your students to say. Is the information:
– true?
– part of a larger context?
– something that everyone knows equally well?
– subject to summary and expansion?
– the source of immediate satisfaction (fun, achievement, competition, etc.)?
– worth talking about?
These characteristics are independent of each other, as the following examples will show:

1. '*The taxi is at the station. Is the taxi at the station?*' '*Yes, it is.*' '*Is it at the hotel?*' '*No, it isn't.*' Here the first sentence stands by itself with no supporting context and so has no truth or falsity. The whole exchange is purely mechanical, probably just part of a drill.

2. '*Is the globe on my desk?*' '*No, it isn't. It's on the bookcase.*' If these exchanges refer to objects actually in the classroom, then the student's replies are either true or false. But a series of such questions do not represent a 'context' for any real-life use of the language, since everyone already knows the facts called for by the questions.

3. *'What is the largest ocean in the world?'* *'The Pacific.'* If this exchange is found in a geography lesson, it is part of a legitimate context and the answer is either true or false. Everyone has equal *access* to the necessary information, which is a matter of public record, but the question still is 'communicative' as one item in a quiz.

4. *'Animal, vegetable or mineral?'* *'Animal.'* This of course is the opening of the familiar game 'Twenty questions.' The answer has truth and is part of the context of a game which is unified by the subject chosen. The information is 'unevenly distributed' because the person who chose the subject knows what it is but the other players don't.

5. *'Is it a six-cylinder car?'* *'No, it's four cylinders.'* This exchange could come from an interrogation about a vehicle known to one of the parties but not to the other – perhaps a prospective buyer and seller. The information is true or false, is found in a legitimate context, and is unevenly distributed. But it is essentially a part of a list, which cannot be expanded without further questioning and which cannot be summarized without loss.

6. By contrast we can summarize a story or a lecture and lose only detail: if it were a shirt we could shrink it without cutting one of the sleeves off. We can also expand such a text by drawing on what we know about the kinds of people and events that it contains.

7. Some exchanges are satisfying regardless of truth, falsity, context, or any of the other characteristics illustrated in 1–6: choral recitation of material with a strong rhythm, or playing the game in which any number related in any way to seven is replaced by the word 'buzz,' or listening to a folk story are three common examples.

8. Some students are frankly not interested in world events or are not charmed by folk stories, or think that counting '13, buzz, 15, 16, buzz, 18 . . .' is a waste of time. All of the first five factors put together cannot guarantee that a given class or a given student will consider a given activity to be worth doing.

So much, then, for the general concepts. In the rest of this chapter we'll look at a series of techniques that you can use to lead your students across the desert that lies between the sterile security of memorizing and drilling, and the satisfaction of genuine, spontaneous communication with speakers of the language who are not their teachers. Over the decades and the centuries, language teachers have invented (and sometimes forgotten and reinvented) hundreds and hundreds of techniques. For this book I have selected a few of the most widely-used and a few less common ones which I hope will stimulate your imagination. As in the earlier chapters I will emphasize both the procedures themselves and the choices that you must make as you follow them.

12.3   Oral activity in the classroom: the teacher's questions

Of all the techniques available to you for moving your students toward real conversation, your own questions are the quickest and easiest. True, they do lack contextual legitimacy because in real life we don't quiz people about what we have just told them. Even so, your questions can call for truth in answers that are based on an established context, sometimes asking a student for information that neither you nor the other students have. You can also use them in ways that build up a vigorous and steady rhythm of activity, or that inject humor into the class, or that contribute toward an atmosphere of mutual trust and acceptance among the people in the classroom. Let's look first at the mechanics of asking questions and then at some of the things you can do with them.

We have already talked about variations in speed, order, loudness and manner in drilling pronunciation and grammar. These choices are also present for you when you ask questions of your students. Your manner is particularly important now that you are actually exchanging information with them. Try to keep it from conveying the unspoken message, 'Now let's see if you can give a sensible answer to this one without making any mistakes.' Let your face, voice and body language imply that you are interested in the students and what they are saying, even when you and they both know that you already have the information.

A second set of choices is available to you when you are asking questions. They depend on the kind of answer that each question calls for, and on the relationship of that question to what the class has been studying.

First, let's look at the kind of answer that you ask for. To oversimplify a bit, there are questions that call for a yes–no answer: 'Is Kinshasa in Zaire?' Then there are those to which the student can reply by merely echoing one of two alternatives that you supply within the question itself: 'Is Kinshasa in

Ghana, or in Zaire?' Finally there are questions to which the student must reply by coming up with some information which is not contained within the question: 'Where is Kinshasa?' If we look at nothing but the linguistic resources which a student needs in order to give the shortest possible correct answer, then yes–no questions are clearly easiest. They require the student only to understand what has been asked and to pronounce one of two easy and familiar words – 'yes' or 'no.' From the same point of view, alternative questions are next simplest because the student can answer such a question by merely repeating the appropriate fragment from what he has just heard. Some question-word questions are usually harder than others in this respect – the answer to a why-question may demand more imagination and richer resources of vocabulary than a who-question or a where-question, for example, but in the chart on p. 124, I've grouped all question-word questions together.

As I said, this ordering of question types from easiest to hardest takes into account only the linguistic resources which they require. Insofar as questions test memory for content of a particular story or bit of exposition, alternative questions may sometimes be easier than yes–no questions. And to the extent that interest contributes to easiness, the grammatical form of the question is of course irrelevant.

A second set of distinctions depends on where the student goes in order to find the answer. If the questions are over a paragraph that describes the Snyder Family, 'How many children do the Snyders have?' can probably be answered by using words taken directly from the paragraph. 'Is Mary Snyder old enough to go to school?' draws on information from the paragraph, but not on its actual wording. 'How many children are there in your family?' may bring an answer that uses wording from within the paragraph, but the information must come from outside it. If you match these two sets of choices against each other, you have a grid with nine squares in it.

Another choice that you must make when you ask questions is the grammatical form that you will accept in the answers. The question 'Is Mary ten years old?' for example, may bring any of the following: 'Yes.' 'Yes, she is.' 'Yes, she is ten (years old).' 'Yes, Mary is ten (years old).' The last two answers are of course rare in real conversation. When we do use them, their function is often to express either weariness or sarcasm. In a language class, however, they are unlikely to be misunderstood, and they at least allow for a kind of direct imitation of a part of the question

	yes–no	alternative	question-word
A: information and words of answer are in the text	Is Mary ten years old?	Is Mary ten years old, or eleven?	How old is Mary?
B: text contains the information needed but not the words	Is Mary old enough to go to school?	Does Mary go to school on Mondays or does she stay at home?	What does Mary do on Mondays?
C: text does not contain the information needed	Have you any children?	Are your children boys, or girls?	How old are your children/sisters and brothers?

in a way that can help to build fluency. The first two answers are definitely more common in English usage, though a plain 'yes' may be a bit abrupt. What is most important is not that you choose one or another type of answer for your students to give, but that you have clear in your mind the reasons for your choice, and that you see how that choice fits in with your goals for the class.

For that matter, this list of four forms is only a language teacher's timid sampling of the replies that English speakers actually give to this type of question. A few of the other possibilities are: 'Yeah.' 'Ten. Yes, she's ten.' 'Right. Ten.' 'I think so, yes.' 'Mhm.' You may decide to show these examples to your students and encourage them to use them. Or you may not. In making this choice as in making the other choices that I have set before you, you need to appear to move from one alternative to another confidently and smoothly. Otherwise your students will quickly become uneasy. Until you have accumulated some experience, therefore, I suggest that you select just a few of the possibilities and polish your use of them before you go on to add others.

Your questions can vary as much in their purpose as in their form. I know several teachers who use rapid-fire questions with full-sentence answers as a very effective means of building fluency: 'Is Mary ten years old?' 'Yes. Mary's ten years old.' Questions which can be answered from the content of a story but not from its wording are a means of encouraging students to form mental pictures of what they hear or read, and of giving them an opportunity to use these mental pictures as a source for what they say. Probing questions can do the same for creative thought, and can also lead to development of deeper relationships among the people in the classroom.

Instead of asking the questions yourself, you can put them into the mouths of your students: 'M, ask N what time he got up this morning.' and so on. Many teachers have made regular use of this technique for decades or centuries. An advantage is that it is one simple way of getting into your students' mouths words that they might not have put there themeslves. A disadvantage is that it can become nothing but that – another case of something 'going into their ears and out their mouths without disturbing anything in between.' You can rescue it from dullness if you choose clever questions and ask them in a way that builds excitement, suspense or humor as the exercise moves along. This technique is sometimes called 'directed dialog.'

There's one thing that you have to be careful about if you decide to use directed dialog. In moving from your cue to his own question, the first student often has to make certain grammatical changes. If your cue is: 'M, ask N where she lives.' the proper response is not: 'Where she lives, N?' but: 'Where do you live, N?' The complexity of these changes varies from language to language. If they're likely to cause serious trouble, you'd better avoid directed dialog altogether. At the stage when your students have begun to deal with the grammatical points that these changes require, you can use directed dialog as one more form of 'transformation drill' (chapter 10) on exactly those points. After they've mastered the mechanics, of course, you can go ahead and use directed dialog freely for other purposes.

In recent years many teachers have begun to use a group of techniques that go under the general name 'Values clarification.' The central component of these techniques is skillful use of teacher questions. Their distinguishing feature is that the questions are about the students' (and the teacher's) own feelings, preferences and beliefs: 'Which would you rather have as a gift, a new bicycle or a good guitar?' 'What is your favorite food?' Anyone is free to decline to answer any question, of course. But if you are sensitive and a little astute in your questioning, you will find that this technique has several strong points: (1) Each student's answer is *factually* correct, and so contributes toward a feeling of dignity, self-esteem, and acceptance in your eyes and in the eyes of the rest of the class. (2) Students can draw much of the vocabulary and grammar for their answers from listening to (or reading) your questions. This fact contributes to the linguistic side of their security. (3) The personal nature of the information guarantees that they will give to it a higher quality of attention than they would give to comparable answers that they found in a book (chapter 1).

You can ask your questions in the form of a list: 'Which of the following would you prefer to do on a rainy weekend: play cards, watch T.V., listen to music, read, (etc.)?' You can then ask members of the class questions about one another's preferences. This allows added practice of the language without reducing the degree of interpersonal involvement. You can use such questions immediately, or the following day, or both.

In an extension of this technique, the students divide into small groups according to their preferences. This allows for physical activity to break up the routine of sitting in the same place throughout the whole class period. Another advantage is that students always know that they are moving into a group which will be congenial – at least with regard to the issue of the moment! While the students are in these groups, you may want to assign them a brief task that is related to the item that they have chosen: 'Now work together and draw up a list of the things you like about playing cards,' for example.

This last activity is a good example of what I meant about balancing the wings of the airplane against each other and gradually making them larger. You chose your original question on the basis of something that the class had already studied – perhaps a dialog or a story. By asking your question you are providing a lively kind of practice on some part of that basic material. But as the groups put together statements of their reasons for their preferences, they are generating new texts – short, but full of life for their authors. These new texts are perfectly suitable for further linguistic exploration and practice. You may decide to use them in this way, or you may decide against it. The thing to be aware of here is that you can change directions and *move back and forth between meaningful text and systematic practice*, starting with either and ending with either.

If your class is reading a fairly long story, your questions can do more than provide 'language practice.' They can also help to bring the story more fully to life. It all depends on how you choose them. The following are typical of questions that the students can answer by referring to the words of the text: Describe the village of Elberon. Who was Charles Blanken?

What did Anna do when she received the letter? These are sometimes called 'comprehension questions.' Indeed, all they do is provide a check on understanding of the story, and an opportunity to use language as a means of verifying that understanding. This activity is therefore predominately a verbal exercise and can be relatively dull.

Is there some way in which we can enlist the students' personalities more fully in answering questions about a story, without at the same time placing a greater burden on their control of the language? The principle of the 'Values clarification' exercises which I have already described will work here too: to tie simple and systematic linguistic structures to the students' feelings, judgments and preferences. Answering these questions – What do you like about Elberon? What would you dislike about it if you lived there? What are the first three things you remember about Charles Blanken? What did Anna do when she received the letter? Do you think she was wise in doing so? – requires virtually the same resources as answering the first set of questions. At the same time, however, they increase the personal involvement of individual students and also provide a starting point for interaction among the students.

But you needn't confine your questions to what the class has already read. Questions about the next section of the story – Do you think Charles will tell Anna the secret? Will they really leave Elberon forever? What should Charles do next? – can both prepare the way – 'break up the sod' – in the language, and stimulate imagination. Having once invested themselves in their guesses, students will give to the rest of the story a superior quality of attention. It has become in some sense 'theirs.'

12.4 Conclusion

These, then are a few of the ways in which you may employ your own questions in order to start your students on the road toward genuine conversation. The two-line exchanges which you initiate with questions will be short and relatively safe from the danger of linguistic error. Perhaps most important, *the interpersonal relationship* between you and your students which they will sense in the exchanges *may either kill their taste for speaking the language, or whet their appetites for more.*

13 Ways to oral activity: games

13.1 Introduction

'What for?' This question is always somewhere in the mind of every one of your students. You as teacher cannot afford to ignore it, for it is the key to motivation and without this food the language-learning turtle (chapter 1) can not walk very far. In chapter 1 we looked at some of the goals that cause students to enroll for language instruction. Those goals are the big, the long-range 'for-whats' of your course and you can't do without them. But they are the hoped-for banquet at the end of a long hike. Your hikers also need snacks and water to sustain them along the path. Long-term goals aren't very helpful here. For short-term, day-to-day motivation your students need many experiences which reach satisfying completion within some framework which is much, much smaller than preparation for a career or for some examination. You will find that games are a rich source of such experiences.

I used to think that games were merely enjoyable activities which I could bring in when I saw that my students were tired from the 'hard work of learning' and needed a change of pace. That was true as far as it went, of course, but there is much more to a game than that. Before I go on to describe some specific and very useful games, let's look at some of the things that we know about games in general.

First of all, people who want to play a game together have to have certain things in common – a chessboard or a playing field, for example. They also share some abilities – the ability to count or to spell or to run, for example. In a language game these shared resources will also include the words and the grammatical patterns that your students know, so you need to have these very clearly in mind as you select or design a game for them. You may base a game on their general background. Or you may choose it for the very precise purpose of bringing to life some new material which they have just finished learning.

A second feature of games is that they have rules. In accepting the rules, the players agree not to do everything that they are physically able to do, but to restrict their actions in certain very clear ways.

A third feature of games is that any restrictions on the players' actions still leave them free enough so that their actions are not entirely predictable. At any point in the course of the game, a player takes into account what the other players have done – what choices they have made from among their options. The player then chooses one of the options that are available to her at that point. Other players respond in the same way to her choice, and so on until the end of the game.

A fourth feature is that the game has a goal. In a competitive game like chess or football the goal is to win by defeating an opponent. In a noncompetitive game like 'Twenty questions,' all players work together in order to bring light out of darkness or order out of chaos. The experience of doing just this is one of the simple, short-term 'for-what's' that I have been talking about.

13.2   A preposition game

Once you become accustomed to working with cuisenaire rods, you will find that there is no end to the games that you can devise with them. Here is one which you can use with beginning students for the practice of prepositions. Divide the students into groups of two or three. Give each group a few rods, with the number and colors of the rods being identical from group to group. One group is to serve as originators, the others as copiers. Stand a notebook or other tall object on the table so that the copiers cannot see the originators' rods. Then place the originators' rods in some kind of configuration which is not visible to the others. The originators describe the configuration and the other groups try to duplicate it. Either you or a student appointed by you watches the work of the copiers and announces when one group has won.

This game is simplest when the originators can see what the copiers are doing and when both sides are free to speak, so that the originators can answer the questions of the copiers. In a more challenging version, the originators are unable to watch the work of the copiers. Most demanding of all, and suitable only for very advanced students, is the version in which the originators cannot see the copiers and the copiers are not allowed to ask questions. In an additional variation, the originators put together their own configuration rather than working from one that you set up for them. The complexity of the task may of course vary from an extremely simple one with only two rods to an elaborate one with as many as ten.

In any of these versions the basic characteristics of a game stand out: the background for activities is the students' shared knowledge of the names for the colors and of simple ways of describing locations. The information about the desired configuration is in the hands of one group but not the others. The simplest way to share that information would be to let everyone see the originators' configuration, but that is ruled out. The words of the originators and the actions of the copiers are unpredictable, and the goal of the game is to match them to one another.

This game illustrates two other general points. The first is the difference between work by individuals and work by groups. I have already reminded you of the fact that human memory is so constructed that an individual can recognize more than she can remember. In a group of three working together, the chances of at least one member coming up with the correct word or grammatical construction is much greater than the chance of any one member of the group coming up with it. If one member suggests a correct wording and another member suggests an incorrect one, the consensus of even a very small group is likely to be right. Even if it is wrong, there is psychological safety in numbers. Competition between groups can be at least as stimulating as competition between individuals and at the same time less threatening.

The second point is that what some people call 'contextualization' is not the same as communication. Take the same rod structures that you used in this game. If you set them up on the desk for the class to look at and then talk about them ('The blue rod is on top of the yellow rod.' 'The yellow rod is under the blue rod and next to the green rod.') or if you ask questions about what everyone can see ('Is the blue rod on top of the yellow rod, or under it?' 'Where is the green rod?') you are providing an experience which is consistent with the words, and words consistent with what your students see, but neither the language nor the visual configuration adds anything to the other. That is to say, your students do not know any facts after you have spoken that they didn't know before you began. They may know some new words, of course, and that's one of the genuine and important values in this kind of activity. But this should not be confused with communication, because there is no transfer of information.

Suppose that instead of a few cuisenaire rods you set before the class a gasoline engine or a painting. If you explain the working of the engine or if you point out to your students something about the painting which they had not noticed for themselves, then there has been communication but no game.

13.3 The Word-card game

This is a surprisingly effective way of helping your students to become comfortable with new vocabulary. Write each target language word on one side of a small card about three by six centimeters. Leave the other side of the card blank. Make a parallel card with an equivalent word or phrase in the students' native language. (Better yet, make a team of students responsible for preparing the cards.) There should be a separate set of cards for every six people.

Begin with a pack which consists of six to ten *pairs* of these cards. Place each card face down on a table in the middle of a group of students. As the game begins, one student picks up any one of the cards, shows it to the others, reads it aloud, tries to give its equivalent in the other language, and returns it face-down to the table. She then does the same thing with a second card. If the two cards happen to match, she removes them from the center of the table, places them in front of her, and takes another turn. If they do not match, the next player takes a turn, and so on until all of the cards have been paired. The player with the largest number of cards 'wins.'

Obviously the way to succeed at this game is to concentrate on the locations of the words as much as on the words themselves. I suspect that this fact somehow helps to account for the effectiveness of the game and for the very positive reactions that it generally draws from students. The quality of the learning that takes place when we focus our attention only on the items to be learned is different from (and probably inferior to) the quality of the learning that is incidental to something else that we are trying to do. That principle applies to all language games, of course, and not just to this one.

In the game as I have described it, any competition that exists tends to be pretty low-key. If a student can't remember the other-language equivalent of the word she has picked up, other students help her. People sometimes give one another hints about the location of the other card in a pair. The game can even be modified so that there is no competition at all within a group. Instead, the group as a whole competes against other groups or against the clock.

One practical hint about this game: don't use many more than ten pairs of cards at one time. Otherwise the mechanical side of the game can become unwieldy and the amount of learning will not be worth the time it takes. But in this as in all other matters, you will have to watch your students' reactions and be your own judge.

13.4 Unscrambling

This well-known game has several variants. To prepare for the game, find or write a short narration such as an anecdote. There should be as many sentences in the text as students in the class (or in each group). Copy each sentence onto a separate slip of paper.

To start the game give one slip to each student. Each student memorizes her sentence and destroys the paper. Then the students repeat their sentences to one another. The object of the game is to put the sentences into the right order and then write the text out in full.

This game requires the students to do more than merely repeat their sentences. They must at the same time pay attention to the meaning of what they are saying and hearing. They will also find themselves talking in the target language *about* the sentences they have memorized – additional and very real practice.

Like the *Word-card game*, this game capitalizes on the fact that students can recognize and understand more than they can produce independently. The particularly nice feature of *Unscrambling* is that is provides virtually all of the language that the students need in order to play it, but the very act of playing forces them to make it their own.

In variations on this game, you can take a comic strip with the words removed. Give the words to the students separately and let them match language to pictures. This is easier if you leave the pictures in their original order, harder if you cut them apart and present them in random order.

A still more demanding game of this sort begins with one of the comic strips which contain no words at all. Each player receives one frame. She must then find a way to describe it to the other players without showing it to them. As before, the object is to put the fragments back together in the right order and so to understand what the whole strip is supposed to be saying. This game too may lead into written composition if you think that is appropriate.

Here, as in all of these games, your essential functions as teacher are first to set the game up clearly, then to monitor its progress and to act as troubleshooter when needed. You of course serve as guarantor of accuracy, just as you do in all activities, but this does not mean that you have to break up the game with your corrections. (If there are too many errors, you have chosen the wrong game, or you have set it up unclearly, or you need to place additional aids at the disposal of your students.) As an optional role you may participate in the game yourself, not as leader but as just another player. Aside from the interpersonal effects of your participation, you will be giving your students some exposure to a speaker of the language doing something besides teaching.

14 Other ways to oral activity

14.1 Introduction

Gabelentz, a 19th-century German, once observed that 'the best language teacher, for beginners at least, is a talkative person with a limited range of ideas.' He probably didn't mean his dictum quite the way it sounded. (I certainly hope that my readers won't be put off by the prospect of having to choose between intellectual alertness and professional effectiveness!) As a matter of fact, the best teachers of beginners that I have known have been conspicuous for the breadth of their interests. Still there is truth in what Gabelentz said, and that truth becomes more and more important the closer we get to real conversation.

Let's take Gabelentz' formula apart and reinterpret two of its terms. First, what did he mean – or what *should* he have meant – by 'a talkative person'? I think the best interpretation is 'a person who obviously enjoys two-way (and not just one-way) conversations with other people.' This is someone who can be relied on to keep the stream of conversation moving, but without monopolizing it. The second term is 'a limited range of ideas.' Surely Gabelentz must have intended here to protect learners from being overwhelmed by a flood of language which they could not come close to understanding. The essential point is not that you the teacher should *have* a 'limited range of ideas'; it is rather that you should be able to talk with your students *within a vocabulary range* that they can handle. And that as you do so, any new words come back several times so that your students can begin to absorb them.

In chapters 12 and 13 we have already looked at how you can use questions and games in helping people to begin to speak the language you are teaching. Some of the most effective techniques for that purpose fit into neither of those categories. They will be the subject of this chapter.

14.2 Microtexts

The microtext is a device which I first met in a second year German course in 1942, but it must have been old before then. In the years since that time I have heard from numerous teachers who have used it successfully.

A microtext may be something that you read aloud, or something that you have prepared ahead of time, or something that you make up as you go along. It is called 'micro-' because it lasts only 30–60 seconds. The basic steps in the technique are as follows:

1. Read or tell the text three times. Indicate when you are about to start again from the beginning, but otherwise do not pause between readings or tellings. I myself prefer the extemporaneous version of this step, but some teachers feel that doing it without a written text is too risky. An advantage of the extemporaneous way is that the three successive tellings, though alike in meaning, provide small differences in wording.

2. Let the students ask questions in the target language or (if you understand it) in their native language, *for the purpose of clarifying their understanding* of what they have heard. This is not the time for them to ask for further information.

3. Read (or tell) the text a fourth time.

4. Ask questions about the text. Try to pick questions that your students can answer correctly and quickly. Move from easier to more difficult questions as described in chapter 12. Mentally award yourself three points if your question gets a right answer immediately, one point if the answer is correct but hesitant, but no points at all if you have to give help or make a correction. This is a simple form of controlled conversation.

5. Read (or tell) the text a fifth time.

6. Invite students to tell one brief thing that they remember from the text. Whatever they say, and whether it is entirely correct or not, repeat it aloud *correctly in a non-correcting tone of voice*. Again, you and they are holding mini-conversations.

7. Let a few students try to give the entire text in their own words. Or break the class into groups of two to four and give them a few minutes to put together their own version of what they have heard.

8. Allow questions which call for further information.

9. Talk with the students *about* the text. Depending on the nature of the text, you may discuss how they liked it and why, or

whether they agree or disagree with it, or what it means. This can be full-scale conversation.

You may want to drop the microtext at this point and go on to something else. Or you may want to make a permanent record of it for future reference. If the text came from a printed source, you can have the students write it out in their own words either individually or in small groups. Then let them compare their work with the original. If the text was something you made up as you spoke, write your own version of it while the students are writing theirs and then let them compare theirs with yours. The advantages of doing things this way are that (1) the mental activity and the judgment required in order to compare two versions can provide yet another occasion for real use of the language; (2) it demonstrates to the students that 'different' is not necessarily 'wrong'; (3) you don't have to spend your time going through a batch of papers one at a time and making earnest 'corrections' which most students will either copy mechanically or ignore. Instead, answer questions that students may have about whether a particular wording is wrong or merely different. In this way you can maintain at a comparatively high level the 'investment' that we talked about in chapter 1.

If you feel like engaging in a little amateur histrionics, you can end the session by going through the text once more extemporaneously, apparently having great trouble with your memory. Each time you pause and look lost, the class 'helps' you. In this way you can arrange for the students to produce either the conspicuous words like nouns and verbs, or the little troublesome words like articles and prepositions. You may even decide that it's worthwhile to pull this trick twice, once for the bigger words and once for the smaller ones. This bit of technique takes advantage of one of the features of memory that we talked about in chapter 4: a student can produce the same missing word from remembering what he heard a minute ago, or from applying a rule that he has memorized, or from drawing on his acquired feeling for the language. In an exercise like the one described in this paragraph, two or three of these processes go on side by side, with the stronger reinforcing the weaker.

The microtext procedure can also lead to material for use in the language laboratory. If you record your successive versions of an extemporaneous text as you speak, students can listen and compare the various versions. As they do so, they may want to copy one or more of the versions onto paper. The overlap of the versions allows for multiple occurrences of most words. It also gives the students valuable opportunities to observe how people speak when they are hesitant, and to compare variant ways of expressing a single idea.

The first seven steps of this procedure should take about 20 or 30 minutes depending on the size of the class. But you may find value in developing a single topic or story into a series of related microtexts.

The liveliness of this technique depends on its flexibility. The first few steps are pretty basic, but after step 5 you may want to skip steps or repeat them or add some of your own. Needless to say, the timing of the move from one step to the next is entirely in your hands. The most important options, however, are in the first step. Watch your students' faces each time you go through the text. If they are uncertain, that's a signal to you not to make many changes in the next telling. If, on the other hand, they seem to be following you very well, you can come back the next time with a noticeably different version of *the same material*.

Finally, two warnings about microtexts, based on the experiences of several of us who have used them: (1) Don't let the text run for more than a minute. If you do, then the rest of the technique will not reach completion in an hour, and may become tiresome. (2) As you go from one retelling to another, don't add much new material. New material will blur the model on which the students must rely in the later steps. Letting yourself go and saying whatever comes into your head may produce an interesting monolog, and it may in fact be highly successful, but you will then be using some other technique, not this one.

To put the same point in terms of that we first met in chapter 4, out of the words that they hear from you in step 1, your students must put together their own nonverbal picture of what you are talking about. Your own first goal is to be certain that they have done so. If you have any doubt, then in your second or third retelling you will stick close to the words you have already used or try to simplify the text still further. Once you sense that your students have the nonverbal picture, there may be value in letting them hear you talk about that same picture in slightly different words. But if you change the words too much, the images from which the students must draw in retelling parts of the text will get in each other's way. You must listen to your own class and balance interest against security.

14.3   Tell and show

Like the *Microtext* procedure, *Tell and show* gives students raw material and then leads them gradually into a conversation. In this procedure, however, the words come (with a little of your help) from the students and not from a book or from a teacher. Again you will want to keep your eye on both wings of the model airplane (chapter 12) to be sure that they stay in balance with each other.

For *Tell and show* you will need a physical medium which is neutral in appearance, highly flexible and simple to use. The equipment that best meets these criteria is, in my experience, a set of the cuisenaire rods (or 'Algebricks') which I mentioned in chapter 7. But perhaps you will find some better vehicle.

In *Tell and show*, one member of the class agrees to serve as originator for the game. The job of the originator is to tell about a place which no-one else in the room has seen. This place may be a distant country or city, or it may be her street or her uncle's house or her room at home. This role gives to the originator absolute power over the facts about which the class will be talking. It also makes her the authority concerning the accuracy of statements made by anyone else in the room – including you! This power-sharing can contribute much toward interest and motivation.

The basic steps in *Tell and show* are:

1. The originator describes the place that she has in mind. She speaks one sentence at a time. With each sentence, she picks out one or more rods and places them on the table in a location that corresponds to what she has just said.

The originator speaks in the target language or in her native language. The important thing here is that she say something significant and interesting. (I cannot emphasize too strongly that this point is essential. If the originator feels obliged to produce nothing but the target language during this preliminary step, she will load herself down with her own linguistic limitations and produce a series of sentences which are as dull as they are safe. Then the procedure will quickly become tiresome to the whole class.) As she speaks and places the rods on the table, you repeat the facts as you have understood them. No matter which language she used, and no matter how many mistakes she made if she used the target language, your repetition is in correct language. Make your manner and your tone of voice conversational rather than 'teacherish.' This means for one thing that you must not convey the unspoken message, 'Be careful! You've just made a mistake!' Such a message is in fact not necessary; most students will pick up most of their own errors in this step just by noticing the differences between what they have said and what they are hearing. On the positive side, your manner can reflect (and even exaggerate) the idea that *you* depend on the *originator* for verifying your understanding of the facts.

Although the originator controls what she says, you still decide how much of it she gets to say. This is a crucially important responsibility. Your goal is to have a total text which will be challenging to your students, but which they can handle in 30–50 minutes. Depending on the strength of the class, this may mean as few as five sentences from the originator or as many as 15 or 20.

2. Tell back in your own words what you remember. As in step 1, you may want to dramatize slightly your dependence on the originator's firsthand knowledge of the facts. Step 2 gives you several valuable opportunities: (1) You let the class hear correct language for a second time. (2) In speaking without interruption, you can now make the language smoother and more idiomatic. (3) You can shift the wording into sentences that are as short and simple as you think appropriate. (4) By feigning absent-mindedness or prolixity, you can provide extra occurrences of any items that you suspect might cause difficulty.

From this point on, you can treat *Tell and show* pretty much as you treated the *Microtexts*. A good third step is delayed free recall of parts of the text that has been created (see step 6 of that procedure) and then recall of the whole text (step 7 of that procedure). From there you can move on to dictation or tape recording or drawing pictures or almost anything else. One thing that you can do here that you couldn't do with *Microtexts*: sweep the rods into a pile at the center of the table and require the students to reconstruct the configuration for the originator but without her help!

If you use a tabletop which is free of books, papers, pencils and other clutter, the simple visual image can stimulate imagination and produce an amazing degree of concentration.

In another variant of this procedure, the entire class (or small group within a class) serves as originator. The subject must then be a place that they all know. The communication centers on reconciling the differences between their memories of it and on deciding how best to represent it with a handful of colored rods.

14.4 Debating

With classes that already control a little of the language, an old-fashioned debate can produce sustained and purposeful use of it. Even though there are only two teams of two speakers each, the entire class can participate in preparing the arguments. After making this kind of investment in the debate, each student will give it high-quality attention. Some of the choices that are open to you are:

– Select the topic yourself, or let the students select it.
– Use a topic that is controversial and frequently discussed outside of class ('Women should carry primary responsibility in caring for children.'), or a topic that requires a little research ('Increased use of coal will produce dangerous changes in the earth's climate.').
– Let the students depend on the language that they already know, or provide them with source material.

Whichever choices you make, it's important that you maintain the structure of the activity: time limits, where the speakers sit, and so on. Otherwise it will turn into nothing but a group argument. A group argument may be just the right thing for some occasions, but it doesn't carry either the clarity or the prestige of a formal debate.

14.5 Appreciating poetry

People are sometimes intimidated by poetry, even in their own native language. For them, the reading of a poem in a foreign language is an esoteric undertaking which they think they shouldn't attempt without at least five or six years of studying prose and grammar. That really depends on the poem, though, doesn't it? There are certainly enough English poems that are beyond me! But there are also some interesting ones in simple language. Here are two:

> In firelight
> all of us sat down together,
> spoke without holding back our thoughts –
> either our first thoughts or our deepest.
>
> The ashes cooled til we could sift them through our fingers.
>
> Then in new morning sun

we stretched and stood
to take our homeward paths,
but found not one.

Frank Gardefoy

This one might lend itself to presentation with four alternative last lines:

and all was one.
but found not one.
and all was good.
soon as we could.

Students could be asked to discuss them and decide which is 'the best' (or 'probably the original') ending. Some simpler questions would be 'Where did you visualize this taking place?' 'How many people did you see?' 'How old are they?' 'Are they men, women, or both?' 'Did they eat or drink anything together?' 'Had they ever seen one another before?'

Since you ask . . .

Big disappointments? No,
I've had none of those.

Middle-sized ones? Some,
sown for the most part by others
but watered and tended, all of them,
by me.

Small disappointments? Oh, yes,
yes, more than I can count, and
more than I could live with.
So because I could not sustain them
they starved – died out,
and I died back
away from where they were,
leaving that finger-breadth of earth open for
new seeds.
(New weeds?)

Carol Wilding

This poem opens the way for students to draw on some of their own negative experiences and think about their reactions to them. In leading a class in the study of this kind of poem, you may want to use some or all of the following activities:

Understanding the writer

　1. Working on the language

　Silent reading by the whole class.

— Reading aloud by you.

— Members of small groups try to clarify for one another the literal meanings.

— You answer as best you can the question which the students were unable to answer to their own satisfaction.

　2. Sorting out the ideas.

— In small groups, talk about what the author was trying to say. On how many levels of meaning was she saying it?

— In the same small groups, write a paraphrase of the poem.

— Share the paraphrases between pairs of groups or with the whole class.

　3. Discuss how the author probably felt as she was writing, and the reasons why the students think she felt that way.

Understanding one another

Invite your students, in small groups or in the whole class, to explore their own:

　1. feelings: How do you feel after reading this poem? What in the poem makes you feel that way?

　2. ideas: Do you agree with the ideas in the poem? Why, or why not?

　3. related experiences: What does this poem remind you of? Can you provide illustrations that agree with, or that contradict, what the author was saying?

This activity calls for the students to make personal investments in the discussion on several levels at once. For this reason, I would suggest that you try to avoid the usual 'teacher' image, and concentrate instead on being just an 'understander' and occasional 'clarifier.' That is to say, your words and your manner should not convey 'I'll give you the correct interpretation,' or 'Very good!' or 'No, that's not quite right.' Instead, repeat each student's contribution with interest, partly to be certain that you have indeed understood it, partly to give the class a chance to hear it a second time in correct language, and partly because doing so is a way of giving the student moral support and helping her to continue. Give your own answers to questions only as a last resort.

14.6 Role playing

So far, the techniques that I've described in this chapter have had the students talking as themselves. Any technique which does this guarantees at least a certain amount of realism in communication. But realism in itself is only a means to an end. That end is that the words from the left side of the brain should be matched with rich and lively images on the right side, and that both should lead to some recognizable result. You can also evoke rich, lively and purposive use of language when students are playing the role of fictitious characters. Let's look at four ways of organizing this sort of conversation practice.

1. *Him Tarzan you Jane* The students who are to participate in the conversation are given little except the names of their roles: 'M, you be a traveler, and N will be the ticket agent.' This sort of direction requires the participants to start with a very minimal image and suggests no purpose toward which they are to move as they talk. If is hardly surprising that under these circumstances the conversations that come out are often more perfunctory than animated. The image at the end of the exercise isn't much more vivid than it was at the beginning, and the purpose has remained pretty much, 'OK-let's-string-some-words-together-to-satisfy-the-teacher.' The Tarzan–Jane type of direction simply doesn't provide sufficient structure for many people. On the other hand, a pair of students who are already imaginative may generate a conversation which is quite animated and has a clear dramatic structure.

2. *You say and then she says.* A second type of direction for role playing goes to just the opposite extreme as far as structuring is concerned. It is in fact nothing but a 'directed dialog' (chapter 12) with all of the information given in a single paragraph:

> Tell the ticket agent that you want to go to Philadelphia. She asks whether you want to go by Metroliner or by regular train. You say you think you'll go by Metroliner this time, and ask when the next one leaves. She says the 2:00 train is full, but . . .

I used to think that this sort of exercise spelled things out in such full detail that it was a waste of time. It was nothing but dictation disguised behind a thin veneer of indirect discourse! A number of times, however, sitting and watching students, I've realized that, thin as it may have been, the indirect discourse was providing just the degree of detachment that allowed them to feel that they were generating the conversation for themselves even while they drew as heavily as necessary on the prompts that it was providing to them.

In preparing this sort of material for your students, you can write it so that either (a) the wording of the instructions is an obvious and familiar translation of material that they know well in the target language, or (b) the wording of the instructions determines the content of what is to be said but without giving a close model for its form:

> You meet a friend who has been ill *and ask how she is feeling today.*

or

> You meet a friend who has been ill *and inquire after her health.*

3. *Cross purposes* Each participant knows in general what the other's role is, but each has a set of specific instructions unknown to the other:

> You are spending a few hours in Lisbon and would like to practice your Portuguese. You stop at a souvenir shop to buy a picture postcard, hoping to interrogate the vendor about the pictures before you buy one.

> You are the proprietor of a souvenir shop in Lisbon. You have just received a shipment of ornamental tiles with pictures of life in Portugal. Since you bought them at a very low price, you stand to make a nice profit on every one you sell.

You have given – or lent – to the participants enough image and enough purpose to get them started. This makes things easier than *Him Tarzan you Jane*, while allowing for a more lively conversation than *You say and then she says*.

4. *What if!* Borrow two characters with whom your students are already familiar. They can come from a play, a short story, a novel, a movie, history, or even from the students' circle of acquaintances. You thus start with a readymade set of well-developed images. Your contribution is to provide a new purpose: Horatio and Ophelia discussing their mutual friend Hamlet; Maxwell Smart and Agent 99 gossiping about James Bond; you and another teacher talking about your jobs; Santa Claus in conversation with an air traffic controller or a customs agent.

5. *More involved role plays* If you have time you can produce background material and roles which result in a class or group

discussion providing several hours of language practice (including preparation of ideas and language, the role play itself and follow-up work). There are many published materials which do this for you. Full-scale simulations are also becoming increasingly popular in language classrooms.

14.7 Conclusion

To summarize these last three chapters, then, getting a conversation going in a foreign language class is something like building a fire in a wood stove. First you have to be sure the fuel is dry and where it needs to be. There's a place for the small kindling and a place for the larger sticks and a place for the logs, and things won't go very well if any of these is out of its place. Similarly, you want to ensure that the necessary words and images are available to your students, and you are responsible for giving a clear overall structure to the activity. The gathering and laying of the fuel are like 'control' as I used that term in chapter 1. But fire also needs air – what in the same chapter I called 'initiative.' If you blow too much air over the fire too soon, it will go out. Later on, though, if you don't let it have enough air you will smother it.

I have listed but a few of the ways of involving your students in oral activity. Each teacher will develop his own methods suitable for his class. However, there are many excellent source books for ideas, which you will want to consult. I refer to some of these in chapter 21.

15 Writing for your own students

15.1 Introduction

In the chapters on techniques, I have emphasized your role, the choices that are open to you, and your responsibility for making them even when you are following a published textbook. In most of your teaching you may be required to use existing books. It's probably best to do so anyway, at least until you've accumulated a little experience. But there will come a time when you feel that the needs of your class are very clear, and that you understand those needs, and that nothing available in print quite meets them. So you will sit down and write something for tomorrow's class. As you write, you will begin to develop certain skills: the skill of seeing your own words in several different ways at the same time, and the skill of guessing how your students will react to what you are putting together for them.

The purpose of this chapter and of chapter 16 will be to give you a little preliminary practice in a few of those skills, and, by giving you practice, to begin to show you what they are. So you may just read through these two chapters if you like, but I think you will understand them better if you actually do the exercises – best of all if you do them in the company of a few other teachers.

15.2 The 74-step exercise

One of the most useful assets you can have is the ability to appreciate how small an increase in grammatical structure can be and still cause trouble for your students. The best way to develop this ability is to guide a class through a series of lessons in which the introduction of new grammar and vocabulary has been strictly controlled. One of the most valuable experiences I had as a new teacher consisted of doing just that using Fries,

Kitchin and French's *English through practice*, now long out of print. A few years after that – and many years ago now – I wanted to give to a group of trainee teachers some feeling for what that experience had been like. So I put together the following 74-step exercise. Although this exercise may appear a bit rambling and ungainly, a surprising number of teachers have found it useful.

The '74-step exercise' has a twofold purpose: to present to you one by one some of the common word classes and constructions of the English language, and to give you practice in writing within narrow restrictions of grammar and vocabulary. As you grow more and more accustomed to *writing* within restrictions, you will find that you will become able to do the same in *speaking* with your students. When you can do this and still *sound* as though you're speaking naturally, you will have gained control of one of the most powerful tools a language teacher can wield.

In order to do this exercise, you will need a picture that tells a definite story.

1. First of all, choose six 'count nouns' that you think will be useful in telling an interesting story about your picture. A count noun is a word which ordinarily occurs in the frame 'two ....s': 'two *houses*,' 'two *cities*,' 'two *cups*,' etc., and does not occur in '............ is good.' A 'mass noun,' by contrast, is one which functions like 'milk' or 'sugar,' as in 'two *cups* of milk,' 'three *pounds* of sugar.' List your six count nouns.

2. Write out each count noun with 'a' or 'an.' You now have a total vocabulary of eight words.

3. Now take the word sequence (not 'construction') 'This is.' Write it out with all the constructions from step 2 above. By this stage your student has a total repertoire of six complete sentences.

4. You may now substitute 'that' for 'this.' Total repertoire has jumped to twelve sentences. 'This' and 'that' are members of the same word class.

5. Now, with no addition of new vocabulary, try switching the positions of 'this'/'that' and 'is.' This gives you twelve brand-new sentences, different from all that have gone before. You recognize them as questions. In English this arbitrary way of signaling that we are asking a question is very important. Furthermore, it seems quite foreign to students from many language backgrounds.

6. Add 'yes' to your vocabulary.

7. Add 'it,' in the sentence 'It is a ....' Total repertoire is now thirty-one sentences.

8. 'Yes, it is.' Note that we can omit the noun phrase in a short answer like this.

9. 'No.' Notice that 'yes' and 'no' belong to a word class with only these two members.

10. 'No, it isn't.'

11. Next, add the plurals of the six count nouns in step 1. Note that your students now have to learn that these plurals cannot follow 'a' ('a house,' etc.). Note also the difference in pronunciation of the plural endings in words that end with different sounds: 'dish' has /dɪʃɪz/ 'dog' has /dɒgz/, 'duck' has /dʌks/.

12. 'These are ....s.'

13. 'These' may be replaced by 'those.'

14. 'Is' may be replaced by 'are.' Note the very important fact of agreement in number among 'this'/'these,' 'is'/'are,' 'a'/'..........,' and 'house'/'houses.' In English this is an important signal for showing which words go together as subject and verb.

15. 'They are ....s.' At this point note the extra dividend: adding no further constructions and no further vocabulary, you get eighteen new sentences of the type 'Are they ....s?' 'Yes, they are.'/ 'No, they aren't.'

16. Add 'I'/'we'/'you'/'he'/'she.' Note how these words pair off with 'is'/ 'am'/'are.' Use them in the sentences of steps 1–15.

Now, using the picture you have chosen, write as interesting a 'story' or dialog as you can, remaining within the limits in steps 1–16. An example of what others have done within these limitations is given below, in connection with a picture which shows a pair of newlyweds in a car behind a school bus. (Note well that the point of this exercise is *not* to produce usable materials. What you write will very likely turn out to be fragmented in content and unnatural in style. The purpose of this activity is to practice working within a series of limitations which are both narrow and strict.)

A: Is this a bus?
B: No, it isn't. It is a car.
A: Is that a man?
B: Yes, it is.
A: Is this a man?
B: No, it isn't. It is a woman.

17. You may now add the word 'not,' as used with the various forms of 'be.' At this point you would have to show

where 'not' is located relative to the verb and to other words, both in statements and in questions, and to teach use of two sets of contractions ('he's not' versus 'he isn't').

18. Add three qualifying adjectives. A qualifying adjective is one that fits into the frame 'It's a very .... thing.' Choose adjectives that will help you make your story interesting. At this point you may also add a seventh count noun.

19. Next, add the construction 'this'/'that' plus a count noun. True, you have already had all these words, but until now 'this' and 'that' have only occurred alone as subjects of sentences.

20. Add the construction adjective plus count noun and put 'a'/'an' before it to form a more complex construction.

21. Use the adjectives alone after forms of 'be.' ('This house is *white*,' etc.)

22. Use 'the' with count nouns, or count nouns plus adjectives.

23. Use a prepositional phrase (e.g. '*in* a basket') after a form of 'be.'

24. Choose two prepositions which you think will make your story interesting. (Some common prepositions are 'in,' 'on,' 'at,' 'to,' 'for,' 'by,' 'under.')

25. Add the word 'and.' Notice that this word joins units of several types: adjectives ('big' and 'red'), count nouns with 'a'/'an'/'the' ('the house' and 'the yard'), prepositional phrases ('in the yard' and 'around the house'), and so forth.

26. Now write a series of questions with 'where': 'Where is the house?' and the like.

27. Next, write some sentences of the form 'There is a .... on the ....' Notice that the word 'there' as used in these sentences is always unstressed, unlike the word which is spelled the same way in 'There he is.'

28. Write some sentences containing 'mine,' 'yours,' 'his,' 'hers,' 'its,' 'theirs,' 'ours.'

29. Write some sentences containing 'my,' 'your,' 'his,' 'her,' 'its,' 'their,' 'our.'

30. You may now start using possessive forms of nouns. Three things to remember: first, there is a variation in pronunciation similar to the one we noticed for the plurals in step 11; second, the use of the apostrophe in writing possessives is a separate teaching problem; third, many nouns which stand for inanimate things use a prepositional phrase with 'of ....' rather than the possessive form with '............'s.'

31. Write a sentence of the form 'The .... is ....-ing now.'

32. Choose any four verbs. Note that at this stage they will have to be 'intransitive' verbs; that is, they will have to be verbs that don't need to have nouns following them. Some intransitive verbs are 'work,' 'walk,' 'talk,' 'sleep,' 'smile.' Using whatever you can from the vocabulary and grammar in steps 1–30, write sentences with these verbs. Now write the most interesting dialog or commentary you can about the picture you have chosen. Here is a further example:

> This a bus. It is a large bus. These are students. The students are in the large bus. They are not in the car. They are laughing.
>
> This is a man. That is a woman. This is a new car. These are new suitcases. They are in the car. The man and the woman are in the new car. The man is driving. The man and woman are happy.

33. Write a sentence of the form 'The .... has been ....-ing.' Note that the choice of 'has'/'have' depends on your choice of singular or plural count noun as subject.

34. Choose two more intransitive verbs and use them in sentences like those in steps 31 and 33.

35. Now choose four more verbs – transitive ones this time. Some verbs that are usually transitive are 'see,' 'hear,' 'understand,' 'throw.' Write sentences using these verbs with count nouns as their direct objects.

36. Now, by reversing the order of subject and certain auxiliary verbs, notice that you can create 'yes'–'no' questions: 'Has he been ....-ing?' 'Is he ....-ing now?'

37. Use 'not' with the statements and questions in steps 31, 33, 36. Notice where you have to locate 'not' in each type of sentence. This placing of 'not' is hard for many students from other language backgrounds.

38. Choose any three time expressions – words or groups of words – that are compatible with 'He is ....-ing.' (You have already had one: 'now.') Use them with your stock of verbs. Make the time expressions as long and complex as you like, but remember that you may not alter them by one word in the remainder of this exercise! For example, 'at this very moment.'

39. Choose any three time expressions that are compatible with 'He has been ....-ing'; e.g. 'since you were here last week.'

40. Now write some sentences with the so-called 'simple

present' form of some of your verbs. Notice the differences in meaning signaled by such differences in form as 'He walks to school (every day)' versus 'He is walking to school (now).' Note also the choice of 'walk'/'walks,' depending on what word is subject of the verb.

41. Choose three time expressions compatible with the simple present forms of verbs.

42. Change some statements with simple present verbs into questions that can be answered by 'yes' or 'no.' What formal changes did you make in the statement to signal this difference in meaning?

43. Do the same with 'not' plus some 'simple present' sentences. The changes you have made in steps 42 and 43 are among the most arbitrary changes in English and are hard for almost all students.

44. Choose three more verbs.

45. Choose three two-word verbs. These verbs should have stress on the second element. Some examples are 'stand up,' 'sit down,' 'set down,' 'put away.'

46. Choose five more prepositions.

47. Write some sentences with the 'going-to' future: 'He is going to wake up,' etc. Notice how you form negatives and 'yes'/'no' questions with this type of verb phrase.

48. Choose three time expressions that you can use with the 'going to' future.

49. Choose five new count nouns, two new conjunctions ('or' and 'but,' probably), and six new qualifying adjectives.

50. Write a new version of your story or dialog.

51. Add the question words 'Who?' 'What?' 'When?' Notice how they affect the order of subject and verb and how they require 'do'/'does' with the simple present form.

52. Now introduce the simple past tense, with its question patterns and negative patterns. Notice the different pronunciation of the 'regular' past ending with 'walk'/wɔːkt/, 'show'/ʃəʊd/, 'pat'/pætɪd/. This should remind you of endings we talked about in connection with step 11. Remember also that many of the most common and most useful verbs form the past tense in an irregular way: 'run' has /ræn/, 'send' has /sent/, 'put' has /pʊt/.

Your student has to learn each of these forms separately. It's a good idea *not* to have him just practice saying 'run, ran; send, sent; put, put.' Instead let him practice them in short but realistic sentences. By so doing he will also be practicing some of the rules which govern the way each verb is used in sentences: 'He runs every afternoon.' 'He ran yesterday.' 'He sends some money every week; he sent it yesterday.'

53. Choose three time expressions that will go with the past forms of your verbs and will also contribute to your story.

54. Write some sentences in which you use 'can' with the simple form of some of the verbs. Note that 'he,' 'she,' 'it,' do *not* require a form '*cans*.' 'Can,' when used in this way sometimes is called a 'modal.' Notice how modals are used in questions or with 'not.' This fact about word order is difficult for most students.

55. Choose three more verbs.

56. Choose two more modals. Some common modals are 'will,' 'could,' 'may,' 'must,' 'might,' 'would,' 'should.'

57. Choose three qualifying adverbs. These should be words that can be used with 'very' in sentences like 'He did it very ....' ('rapidly,' 'well,' 'poorly,' 'cheerfully')

58. Add numerals from one to ten.

59. Add numerals from 16 to 19. Notice how they are related in form to certain numerals from step 58.

60. Add numerals from 11 to 15. Why do these present a special problem not found in step 59?

61. Add numerals from 20 to 100.

62. Now add the words 'some' and 'any,' pronounced with weak stress: 'We need some paper'; 'Do you have any paper?' but *not* 'Any paper will do.'

63. Add 'also,' and 'too' when it is used like 'also.' You are *not yet* authorized to use it with adjectives or adverbs, as in 'too big,' 'too slowly.'

64. Add stressed 'here'/'there.' ('Here is your coat,' etc.)

65. Write some sentences of the form 'The .... has .... the ....' ('The dog has torn the curtain.') Write questions and negative statements with this verb form.

Notice that for many common verbs your students now have to learn a third form ('write,' 'wrote,' '*written*'), whereas for many others no new form is needed ('wait,' 'waited').

66. Choose three time expressions that will go with the verb forms of step 65 and will help your story.

67. Add 'many' and use it in a few sentences.

68. Add 'every' and 'no,' as in 'every child,' 'no child.'

69. Choose three mass nouns which you can use in talking about your picture. (See the first step for a discussion of count nouns.) Some frequent mass nouns are 'water,' 'food,' 'work.'

Note that
although we say: we usually say:

    Count Noun   *Mass Noun*
    a dog   (some) water
    some dogs   some water
    two dogs   two quarts of water
    a few dogs   a little water
    many dogs   much water

70. Add 'much' to your vocabulary.

71. Choose three 'frequency adverbs.' Some of the most common of these are 'often,' 'seldom,' 'sometimes,' 'never,' 'always.' As a group they are distinguished from other adverbs by the position which they frequently occupy between auxiliary verb and main verb: 'I have *never* forgotten your birthday.'

72. Now write a few sentences using 'marked infinitives' – 'to' plus the simple form of the verb: 'I need to buy an alarm clock.'

73. Add four mass nouns, four count nouns, four verbs, and four qualifying adjectives.

74. Now – write as interesting a story as possible relating to your picture. For example:

> A man and his wife are driving along the road very slowly in their new car. They have been married for only a few minutes and have just started on a long trip. They have packed their suitcases and put them in the car. The suitcases are new; the car is also new. The man bought the car only a few days ago.
>
> The man seldom drives slowly but now his car is behind this large bus and he cannot pass it. Whenever the bus stops the car has to stop. While the bus is stopped a car may not pass. The man has to drive slowly.
>
> Many of the children are standing up to see the man and his wife. They have been sitting down in the bus but now they are standing up. They are very curious. The man and his wife are not looking at the children. The children are laughing at them, but the man and his wife do not care. They are thinking about the long trip. They are very happy. The children are happy, too.

This story was written about an illustration taken from a popular magazine.

These 74 steps are of course only one of the many possible

sequences in which this amount of English grammar might actually be presented to a group of students. I would certainly not suggest that it is the best sequence. Its value here is again that of the jungle gym (chapter 1) – a rigid structure within which you can develop your muscles in your own way.

16 Adapting printed texts

16.1 Introduction

There is no such thing as a complex topic. For that matter, there's no such thing as a simple topic, either. The complexity and the simplicity lie in how we treat the topics. Take the subject of nutrition, for example. We can cover it in one very simple sentence: 'Good food brings good health.' We can complicate our treatment just a bit by listing the four (or is it five?) basic groups of foodstuffs. Or we can write a detailed account of the metabolism of certain fatty acids. The same principle applies when we talk or write about people. We can go from 'My father was a tall man. He worked in the post office.' all the way to a full-length psychoanalytic biography or a poem. Sometimes (especially when we don't agree with what has been said) we tell someone, 'But you're oversimplifying!' Whether we're right or not, the point is that in using language we can and do 'boil things down' (or boil them up!) to suit our purposes.

This fact has one very important implication for your work: *You can write about anything with any degree of complexity.* By exploiting this fact you will greatly increase the range of supplementary readings and 'microtexts' that you can make available to your students.

As far as the mechanical side of language is concerned, there are three principal sources of complexity. They are vocabulary, sentence length, and grammatical structures. In this chapter we'll be working with ways to control the last two of these, and particularly the third. Like chapter 15, this chapter will probably mean more to you if you actually write out the exercises that it suggests. The purpose of these exercises is to introduce you to one trick: putting the original words of one long and complicated sentence into a number of shorter and very simple sentences which add up to the same total meaning. This trick sounds simple, and in theory it is. I think you will find, however, that it takes a little practice.

16.2 An example

The concept is illustrated by these three equivalent versions of an anecdote which originally appeared in *Time Magazine* as a single cleverly complex sentence. It has been rewritten into three versions. You will notice that all of these versions employ almost the same nouns, verbs and adjectives, but vary greatly in their grammatical complexity.

Kenneth Muller, version A

1. Kenneth Muller was a little boy.
2. He was three years old.
3. He wanted to learn to read.
4. He wanted to read books.
5. He was young.
6. He could not learn to read.
7. He could not go to school.
8. Three years passed.
9. Kenneth was six years old.
10. He went to school.
11. He was in the first grade.
12. He learned very quickly.
13. He learned to read.
14. He learned to read many words.
15. One of the words was 'pull.'
16. He learned to read 'pull.'
17. One day, Kenneth was in the hallway of the school.
18. There was a red box in the hallway.
19. The red box was on the wall.
20. Kenneth saw the red box.
21. There was a handle on the box.
22. Kenneth saw the handle.
23. There was a word on the box.
24. Kenneth saw the word.
25. The word was 'pull.'
26. Kenneth pulled the handle.
27. The whole school had an unscheduled fire drill that day.

In version A, the sentences are short. Each sentence has only one clause. The verbs are all in the active voice, and I have used only the simplest tenses. I have even done without some common words like 'enough' and 'ever since' because I know that some students have trouble with the grammatical patterns that they require.

Version A is clearly not an example of normal narrative style in English. That is obvious to you, and I daresay it will be obvious even to most beginners in the language. It can do one thing, however, which a more colloquial and more complex version could not do as well. By the very poverty and monotony of its sentence structures, and by the repetitiousness of its vocabulary, version A allows students at a very early stage to feel the thrill of having followed a real story. One teacher whom I have watched many times in recent years gets excellent results with beginners in this way. Perhaps each short sentence is a part of a separate image, and the images tie into or build onto one another.

Even if you decide that version A is not suitable for direct use in your classroom, the ability to make this sort of thing from an idiomatic text can be a useful skill for you in at least three respects. First, these short sentences when combined in a few simple ways can become a much smoother but still easy version B (as we will see in a moment). Second, you can ask the students to combine or change these sentences after you have used the B or C version orally in class: 'Change these sentences to yes–no questions, and then to indirect questions,' or 'Rewrite the sentences replacing nouns with pronouns.' (This last exercise would produce such sentences as 'He wanted to do something.' 'He couldn't do it.') Third, you may find that you can use a few (not all!) of these short sentences for pronunciation practice. For example the sentence *One of the words was 'pull'* contains three examples of the sound *w* at the beginning of words, yet it is hardly what one could call a tongue twister.

You have of course noticed that the last sentence of these 27 is by far the most difficult. If I had maintained the A level of structure, I would have had to replace it by a series of simpler sentences such as:

Bells began to ring.
The teachers heard the bells.
The pupils heard the bells.
They stood up.
They walked out of their classrooms.
They walked through the halls.
They walked carefully.
They walked quietly.
They walked out of the school.

They stood outside the school.
They waited there.
The principal came to the door of the school.
He said, 'The school is not burning.
There is no fire.
Come into the school again.
This was a fire drill.'

(The meaning of 'fire drill' has been given in the sentences that precede this one. To get across the meaning of 'unscheduled,' we may add the sentences that follow.)

The children and their teachers went into the school again.
They began to study again.
The fire drill surprised the pupils.
It surprised the teachers.
It surprised the principal.

Still on the A level, you can ask your students two questions to which they can reply adequately with a *yes* or *no*: Did the fire drill surprise Kenneth? Do you like fire drills? The first of these questions requires your students to make an inference on which they may disagree among themselves. The second allows them to express personal preferences.

Now let's look at a second way of telling the same story:

Kenneth Muller, version B

When little Kenneth Muller was three years old, he wanted to read books. But he could not go to school or learn to read because he was very young.

After three years, when Kenneth was six years old, he went to school. He soon learned to read very well. One of the many words that he learned was 'pull.'

One day, when Kenneth was in the hallway of the school, he saw a red box on the wall. There was a handle on the box, and there was also a word on it. The word was 'pull.' Kenneth read the word and pulled the handle.

The whole school had an unscheduled fire drill that day.

In version B we have taken the sentences of A and joined them together in routine ways. These ways include the use of relative clauses, *and, or, when, after, before,* and *because*. We're still staying away from any but the simplest and most common tenses.

If version C is too hard for your class, you can begin with B. If on the other hand your class feels that C is better suited to them, you can still use B without their even being aware of its existence. It can serve as an alternative for C when you are first telling the story, or as a source of explanatory paraphrases.

Kenneth Muller, version C

Little Kenneth Muller had wanted to learn to read ever since he was three years old. Finally, when he was six, he was old enough to go to school. He soon became the best reader in the first grade.

Among the first words that he learned to recognize was 'pull.' One day, he noticed that word printed on a red box in the hallway of the school. There was a shiny metal handle sticking out of the box. Being an obedient child, Kenneth pulled it.

All thousand children in Kenneth's school had an unscheduled fire drill that day.

If you will take the numbered sentences of A and see what has happened to them in B and C, you will see that there is much more gramatical diversity in C than in the other versions. Some classes would be able to begin right away on C; others need the preparation of A and B. And of course some classes can handle a much more complicated C than others can.

The Kenneth Muller story has provided an example of ways in which you can use one or more rewritten versions of an original story. But when you rewrite, you almost inevitably alter the style of the story into something that reads as though it had been done for a language class. It has, of course, and you needn't apologize for it! There is a time and a place for that sort of lesson material.

If, however, you can preserve the original version, you can realize two advantages. First of all, it contributes to motivation. There's something intrinsically rewarding about the feeling that as a foreign learner one has dealt successfully with a text that was clearly intended for the eyes of natives. Second, it widens the range of styles to which your students are exposed.

16.3 A second example

Here's an example taken from a recent newspaper, on a topic which is of interest to many students of foreign languages:

It was love at first sight. So I told three friends, and they told three friends, and they told three friends. And now standby seats on British Caledonian's new London–Hong Kong flights are as popular as free samples from Fort Knox.

But I guess we're not solely responsible. At only $240, that's the sort of ticket offer that inspires travelers to rise right out of their armchairs. Better yet, there are more peaches on the same tree. In fact, some observers figure that standbys will be the biggest and therefore best deals in international bargain fares this winter, though it's impossible to predict the number of actual seats.

The writing here is of course very colloquial, lively and with figures of speech that may confuse many intermediate learners of English. This is hardly the sort of thing that one would have people memorize and recite. It would come out sounding very stale. I would not recommend it as an immediate oral or written production: asking students to use *love at first sight* or *more peaches on the same tree* in sentences, for example. But I think we can still keep the sprightly writing of the original if we are reasonably shrewd in how we supplement it. One trick is to make a clear distinction between what we ask our students to produce, and what we ask them only to understand.

You can, for example, write a series of multiple-choice questions which will help to clarify the original text. If these questions are at a grammatical level which your students already control, then the questions themselves can serve as models for production (as well as providing extra comprehension practice):

1. By '*love at first sight*,' the writer means:
    a) that she was enthusiastic about the price of a ticket;
    b) that she was in love with one of her three friends;
    c) that her first visit to Hong Kong was a very happy one.
2. By a *free sample from Fort Knox*, the writer means:
    a) a handsome soldier;
    b) a bar of gold;
    c) military discipline.
    and so on.

Another possibility is to prepare a parallel text in the kind of language which your students can write:

I was so enthusiastic about the cheap fare that I told all of my friends about it, and all of them told all of their friends. Maybe that's why Avitrans Airways standby tickets have become so popular. Or maybe it's just the low price. But other airlines are offering comparable bargains. Even so, many people who are familiar with the travel industry say that the regular tourist class ticket will continue to be the best buy.

Notice that this is not a close paraphrase of the original, and that in some details it disagrees with it. You can ask your students to copy it, changing the parts that disagree so as to bring them into accord with the original. They can do this either individually or in small groups.

A third possibility is to be sure that everyone understands the overall meaning of the passage and then use it as a springboard for discussing the meaning of standby in this context. Then pose the questions: Would you fly standby if it cost only one per cent less than the regular fare? What if it cost only 10 per cent of the regular fare? What is the smallest difference in fares that would make it worthwhile for you to fly standby? Let them discuss their answers first in small groups and then in the class as a whole.

PART 3   BEYOND THE CLASSROOM

17   Some basic ideas in phonetics

17.1   Introduction

The first part of this book (chapters 1-5) was about the people in the classroom – you and your students. The second part (chapters 6-16) was about what you do there – the techniques and materials that you use. There's one more ingredient of your job about which you should know something, and that is the language itself. I don't mean to say that in order to be a good language teacher you have to keep up month by month with changing theories of language in general, or with the most recent and logically elegant analysis of the language you are teaching. You should, however, know enough about how language works so that you can watch it at work and be able to keep some kind of track of what you're seeing.

The person whose profession it is to keep track of the workings of languages is the linguist. Although linguists *as linguists* are not particularly qualified to *teach* a language (or to advise others on how to teach it), they can be of considerable help to you in this third aspect of your job. So I suggest that you at least keep in touch with them for the light that their formulations can shed on what you're doing. That light will be helpful if you don't stare at it too directly or too long and so become blinded to the other aspects of your work.

Linguistic theory and scientific analysis of individual languages, like any other scholarly discipline, have their own characteristic raw materials. One can follow the arguments of the linguists and appreciate their conclusions better if one has handled a few of the data from which they are drawn, just as a person who has played a little football in school is better able to see what is going on in a professional game than is someone who has never participated at all.

In chapters 17-20, therefore, we'll look together at some of these basic data. We'll spend most of our time in the areas where linguists have been conspicuously successful in producing neat formulations. These are the study of sounds and the study of sentences. First, though, let's spend just a page or two with some of those parts of human communication that come through channels other than words: through facial expression, body posture, movement or lack of movement, tone of voice and so on. If verbal communication is the pen which spells out details, nonverbal communication provides the surface on which the words are written and against which they must be interpreted.

Some features of nonverbal communication seem to be the same in all cultures: a crying baby is unhappy about something the world around, and wherever you go the basic meaning of a smile is pleasure. Other features vary conspicuously from one society to another: if a high ranking person comes into the room, one custom calls for lesser persons to show their respect by rising, while another custom demands that they sit down.

It is difficult through the *words* of a book to give to one's readers very much experience in working with the raw data of *nonverbal* communication. What I *can* do is to suggest some places where you may look to find such data for yourself in the world around you.

Some of the best-known examples are in the use of time and space. If someone invites you to his home for 'eight o'clock in the evening,' at what time would you actually arrive? What message would you be conveying if you arrived at 7:50? At 8:00 exactly? At 8:10? At 8:30? At 9:30? Not at all? At what point if any would this nonverbal message require a verbal apology? The answers to these questions will vary widely from one culture to another. (In my own native culture they even vary a little from family to family.)

Another well-known example is how far people stand from one another when they are talking to one another. When talking with friends or colleagues a few times tomorrow, try standing a little too close to them (or a little too far from them) and watch for reactions (your own as well as theirs!).

Next, turn on the television if you have one, but leave the sound off. Or watch a movie without listening to what is said. Or just watch real three-dimensional people across the street or on the far side of a restaurant. What can you know – or be fairly sure you know – about them without hearing what they say? Once you have answered that question, try to put your finger on just what signals brought you to that knowledge.

Here are five lines of dialog – five short sentences made up of very common words:

A man came to see you.

Oh? When?

While you were out.

What did he want?

He didn't say.

In your mind's ear, try to hear these lines as they might be spoken by secretary to employer as part of a day's routine. Then listen to them again as they might sound in a movie directed by Alfred Hitchcock. The impact of the same words varies greatly with circumstances!

These few exercises with nonverbal communication will serve as reminders of the setting in which language has meaning, and without which it would not be language. Some linguists have begun the study of new languages by concentrating first on the sounds, and have sometimes organized their accounts as though the languages were made up of combinations (and combinations of combinations) of sounds. The question of whether that was wise is a matter for the linguists to discuss among themselves. For us, however, and for our students, language rises out of – and therefore begins with – what happens between people. Having said that, let's look at a few very basic concepts related to the use of sound in language.

17.2   Some basic concepts

How much do you as a teacher need to know about sounds? There is no exact answer to this question, of course. Maybe the best reply is 'Less than a phonetician but more than your students.' A corollary of this formula is 'Don't tell your students all that you know about pronunciation.' To do so would only burden or bemuse them.

The most fundamental thing to remember in studying phonetics is that you as a *teacher* of languages are concerned not so much with *sounds* as with the *differences between sounds*, and with how each language organizes those differences.

A second fundamental fact is that sounds are not spellings, and that the two don't always match each other. Anyone who has gone through the process of learning to write English knows this all too well: lead (the verb) and lead (the metal) are written alike but pronounced differently, while the latter sounds exactly like the past tense of that verb (led) although it is spelled differently. Those of us who teach English are fond of reminding people of the many pronunciations of *-ough* as in though, through, tough, and so on. If an ideally 'phonetic' language is one in which sounds and spellings match each other exactly, then English (and to a lesser degree French) is an example of a 'non-phonetic' one.

English is, in fact, such a notorious example of a 'non-phonetic' language that people sometimes assume that languages which are more 'phonetic' than English (or French) are entirely 'phonetic.' I was told this at one time or another by the people who taught me German and Russian. As a result, I overlooked the fact that *Rat* (councillor) and *Rad* (wheel) are pronounced alike in German, and I persisted in some rather conspicuous spelling pronunciations in Russian.

If you think your language is 'phonetic' in this sense (and you may be right), ask yourself whether there are any characteristic difficulties which native-speaking children encounter in learning to write. These difficulties often (though not always) lie at points where sound and written symbol don't quite parallel each other.

Actually, this word *phonetic* is used in two quite different senses, and you as a language teacher will need to tell them apart. The popular meaning, which I have already mentioned, I will write between quotation marks. The second meaning, a scientific one, is paired with the term *phonemic*.

We need both of these terms for one simple reason: no two sounds are exactly alike. Pronounce onto tape some simple word such as English *go* or Spanish *yo* (I) twice, trying to make the two occurrences of the word sound exactly alike. Then play the tape back. You may not be able to hear the difference. If you have been very careful, even a skilled phonetician may not be able to tell which is which. But if you run the recording into a sound spectrograph or a good oscilloscope and look at the picture that comes out, you will always be able to pick out minor differences.

As a matter of fact, we're fortunate that our ears *can't* hear such tiny physical differences, for these differences carry no information – they are meaningless. And our brain is so organized that it notices differences that can carry meaning and ignores all other differences.

Some of what the brain learns to ignore consists of differences which it *could* very well hear if it had any use for the distinctions. A well-known example is found in the sounds that are spelled *p* in English *pare* and *spare*. The first *p* is followed by a very definite puff of air, while the second is not. (You can see this difference for yourself by holding a lighted match or a strip of paper in front of your mouth as you pronounce the two words.) In English, the variety with the puff of air never comes directly after *s*, while the variety without the puff of air never begins a word. If you know that one or another of the two is going to come up in a particular place in a sentence, you can always predict which it will be, just by looking at the neighboring sounds. So if you grew up hearing only English, you may have trouble even hearing this difference. These two sounds are part of a group of physically similar but not identical sounds which *in English* are predictable in terms of the nearby sounds. Linguistic scientists call such a group of sounds a *phoneme* of English. In a given language, a phonetic difference which sets apart two phonemes *of that language* is said to be 'phonemic' *in that language*. A phonetic difference between two members of a single phoneme *of a given language* is *not* 'phonemic' *in that language*.

Languages differ according to which physical (and which potentially audible) differences they train their speakers to notice, and which ones they train them to ignore. Much of your work as a teacher of pronunciation will come from the fact that your students, in their experience with their native language(s), have acquired the skill of overlooking differences which they must pay attention to in the language you are teaching them.

The difference between *p* with and without a puff of air, then, is 'not phonemic' in English. That is to say that this difference is never the only thing that sets apart two words that contrast with each other in sound and meaning. (This same kind of difference *is* phonemic in many languages of the world, including Thai, Korean, Zulu, and most of the languages of South Asia.) The difference between the first sounds of *pie* and *buy*, on the other hand, is an example of a feature which *is* phonemic in English. In *pie*, we form the consonant more forcibly than in *buy*, and the vocal cords begin to vibrate a tiny fraction of a second later. (This feature, in turn, is *not* phonemic in some languages.)

In its second, more technical meaning, then, *phonetic* means 'a difference between two sounds seen without regard to whether that difference is phonemic in one language or another.' It is used in talking about speech sounds as physical phenomena. The nontechnical sense, on the other hand, which we mentioned earlier, refers to the overall relationship between the phonemes of a language and the writing system that people use in order to represent them on paper.

Any one language uses only a few dozen phonemes. But even those few phonemes are made up of an even smaller number of 'distinctive features.' Thus the difference between the consonant sounds of *pie* and *buy* is actually the same as the difference between *two* and *do* or between *seal* and *zeal* or between *coal* and *goal*. We will go into greater detail in chapter 18.

So much, then, for the fundamental concepts: *phoneme, phonemic, phonetic* (in two senses) and *distinctive feature*. Let's turn now to some basic information about the physical equipment that we all use in speaking, no matter what our language.

18 The basic equipment for speaking

18.1 The speech apparatus

Much of the mechanical equipment that we use in speaking any language can be seen in a profile view of the head and throat (figure 11). This equipment includes a number of unmovable 'points of articulation' mostly along the top of the mouth, and a number of movable 'articulators' most of which are attached to the lower jaw.

The most important unmovable parts of the speech apparatus are:

Common name	Technical name	Technical adjective
Upper or lower lip	(not in common use)	Labial
Upper teeth	(not in common use)	Dental
Gum ridge	Alveolar ridge	Alveolar
Hard palate	Palate	Palatal
Soft palate	Velum	Velar
Extreme back of soft palate	Uvula	Uvular
Nasal cavity	Nasal cavity	Nasal
Upper throat	Pharynx	Pharyngeal

The principal movable parts of the speech apparatus are:

Lower lip		Labial/Labio-
Tongue tip		Apical/Apico-
Blade of tongue		Blade/Lamino-
Back of tongue	Dorsum	Dorsal/Dorso-
Velic	Velic	Nasal/Non-nasal
Vocal cords	Glottis	{ Glottal { Voiced/Unvoiced
Lower jaw		High/Mid/Low (vowels)

In naming most consonant sounds we have to mention both the articulator and the point of articulation, in that order. So for example a sound in which the lower lip touches the upper teeth

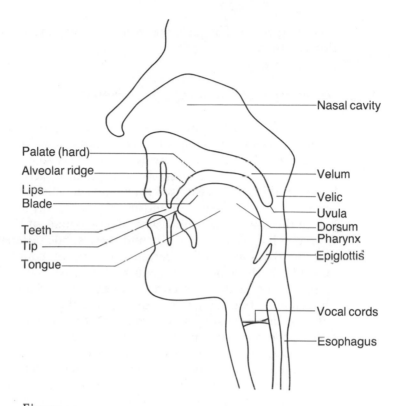

Palate (hard)
Alveolar ridge
Lips
Blade
Teeth
Tip
Tongue

Nasal cavity
Velum
Velic
Uvula
Dorsum
Pharynx
Epiglottis
Vocal cords
Esophagus

Figure 11

is called 'labiodental,' and a 'dorsovelar' sound is one in which
the back of the tongue makes contact with the soft palate.

But the formation of speech sounds doesn't always involve
complete closure between an articulator and a point of articulation. Sometimes the articulator comes only close enough to the
point of articulation so that the air becomes audibly turbulent as
it passes through. Phoneticians call this audible turbulence
'friction'; these sounds are therefore known as 'fricatives.'
Sounds that require momentary complete closure between
articulator and point of articulation are 'stops.' Because both
stops and fricatives involve some obstruction to the airflow, the
two groups together are sometimes called 'obstruents.'

So in English and in most languages the letter *p* (as in *pop*)
stands for a stop sound, while *f* (as in *fife*) stands for a fricative.
Both *p* and *f* stand for obstruents. In German the two occur
together: a complete stop which is released into a fricative, e.g.,

Pfennig (penny). The technical term for this kind of combination is 'affricate.'

18.2   An example of how things get mixed up

Another phonetic feature which is used in English and in many other languages is 'voicing.' Strictly speaking, a 'voiced' sound is one during which the vocal cords are vibrating so as to produce an identifiable (though brief) musical pitch. In actual practice, however, this term is also used for sounds in which the vibration of the vocal cords begins or ends a *relatively* short time after or before the rest of the sound. The precise details of timing vary from one language to another, and these subtle differences can become the source of a certain amount of confusion. For example, both French and English have unvoiced and voiced stops. Moreover the difference between unvoiced and voiced is phonemic in both languages. In English, the word *pie* begins with the unvoiced stop *p*. The voicing of the diphthong which follows the consonant begins relatively late, after a puff of air. As some speakers of English pronounce the word *buy*, voice vibration begins as soon as the lips come together for the consonant. For many other speakers, however, voicing begins later. There are speakers for whom the voice does not begin until the stoppage at the lips has been released. For these people, their consonant in *buy* is actually unvoiced in the physical, phonetic sense. But the voicing still begins sooner than in their pronunciation of *pie*. In this relative sense, their consonant in *buy* can still be called voiced.

Now remember what we said when we were talking about the difference between 'phonemic' and 'phonetic' (17.2): our experience with a language teaches us to notice some differences in sound, but it just as firmly teaches us to ignore – to be oblivious to – certain others. English speakers have long since discovered that one person's fully voiced *buy* means exactly the same as another person's tardily voiced *buy*. As a result, they become very adept at *not* being able to hear or to produce the two sounds in contrast with each other. And that's just fine as long as they're speaking English.

When they try to pronounce French right, it's another matter, at least for the tardy-voicers. French *b* as in *bon* (good) is voiced from beginning to end. French *p* as in *pont* (bridge) is unvoiced, but without the puff of air that we found in English *pie*. The voicing of the vowel can thus begin sooner in *pont* than in *pie*. The voiced–unvoiced contrast, represented in both languages with the letters *b* and *p*, is actually realized in two quite different ways.

One of the practical consequences of this state of affairs is that when a Frenchman speaks English his *p* at the beginning of a word will be close to the *b* of some English speakers. On the other hand, a tardy-voicing speaker of English may find that what he intends as *b*'s come out sounding to the French like *p*'s.

18.3 Another example of 'it is but it isn't'

I've already mentioned how some sounds (most of them stops) are followed by a puff of air. This puff is called 'aspiration,' so that we can speak of 'aspirated' and 'unaspirated' stops. But again, as with voicing, the actual physical realization of aspiration varies from one language to the next. So even though English *p* is aspirated at the beginning of a word – and very strongly aspirated by comparison with sounds that are spelled the same way in Romance languages – English speakers will find that their *p* sound is heard as unaspirated when they try to pronounce some languages which use much stronger aspiration.

All of the features that we have looked at up to this point apply to consonants and (except for the fact that in most languages vowels are voiced) only to consonants. While we're still looking at the profile of the speech apparatus, let's look at the two features that have the greatest effect on what a vowel sounds like. These are the positioning of the tongue from front to back, and the raising or lowering of the tongue and jaw. You will probably be able to feel the back-to-front motion if you pronounce English *law* and then *without letting your voice stop* pronounce *at* or *Ed*. Once you have the feel of your own tongue as it performs this simple task for you, let it move around, and listen to the way the vowel changes as it does so.

In a similar fashion you can get the feel of raising and lowering your tongue by gliding from *two* to *ought*, or from *three* to *at*. Again, unless you've had a course in phonetics somewhere, you may find it worthwhile to experiment a bit with listening and feeling till you get the hang of it. You can hear the sound in an unaccustomed and more vivid way if you face into a corner as you practice. Or make a corner for yourself by holding an opened book in front of your face.

A feature that applies to both vowels and consonants is 'nasalization.' This feature is produced by opening the passage from the mouth up into the nasal cavity. Most people are unable to feel this motion the way they can feel their tongues move. Perhaps this is the reason why you may have been told that in order to produce a nasalized vowel you have to 'talk as though you had a cold in your head.' Exactly the opposite is true: when your nasal passages are blocked by a cold, you *can't* get nasal resonance – you cad't get dasal resodadce – and the *m*'s and *n*'s come out like *b*'s and *d*'s.

One more phonetic characteristic of vowels plays a part in many foreign accents, whether of English speakers learning other languages or of speakers of other languages learning English. This is the difference between 'pure' and 'glided' or 'diphthongized.' To say that a vowel is 'pure' is to say that the tongue and lips move relatively little from the start of the vowel until its end. Both vowels of the Spanish word *reno* are in this sense 'pure.' The so-called short vowels of English are also pure in the standard dialects on both sides of the Atlantic, as in *sit, pat, not, put* and so on. The so-called long vowels of English, on the other hand, are really glides from one vowel-like tongue-and-lip position toward another. The term for such a glide is 'diphthong.' So the vowel of English *no* is heavily glided in comparison with the vowel of Spanish *no*. Similarly the vowel of English *ray* is closer to Spanish *rei* or *reino* than to Spanish *reno*. Therefore English speakers often diphthongize vowels of other languages where the vowels are supposed to be pure. In turn, when speakers of those languages fail to diphthongize a 'long' vowel in English, an English-speaking listener may confuse it with a 'short' vowel: *bait* may sound like *bet* or *note* like *not*, for example.

While we're still looking at the profile, there's another misunderstanding that some non-phoneticians fall into. This has to do with the so-called 'liquid' consonants *l* and *r*. I actually heard one teacher tell his class that because *l* is a liquid, you have to have a good amount of saliva in your mouth in order to pronounce it properly. In fact, the sounds that are spelled with *l* and *r* are consonants that don't require friction or firm closure anywhere. The precise details of how these sounds are formed vary from language to language, and often make up one small but stubborn part of a foreign accent. In general, an *l*-sound requires the tip of the tongue to be placed against some point near the front of the mouth, and the sides to be pulled away from the teeth so that breath can escape past them. These sounds are therefore called 'lateral.' Sounds written with *r* do not have this lateral feature. They consist of a quick tap or flap of the tongue tip against the gum ridge, or of a partial constriction produced by raising the tip of the tongue (American and some other varieties of English) or by placing the back of the tongue near the uvula (standard varieties of French, German and Hebrew). If this constriction is held long enough with just the right degree of tension, it leads to a trill – a rapid vibration either of the tongue tip or of the uvula.

Many languages of the world, including all those of Europe and the Middle East, distinguish between some kind of *r* and some kind of *l*. Therefore when speakers of these languages learn English, their liquid consonants may sound a little foreign, but they don't lead to misunderstandings. In many of the languages of Africa and Asia, on the other hand, only one kind of liquid sound exists, or if both laterals and non-laterals exist the difference between them is not phonemic. This is why speakers of these languages have trouble in hearing and producing the differences between *red* and *led, berry* and *belly, bear* and *bell.*

These are the most important features of speech sounds which show up well on a profile view. Now let's rotate our point of view by 90 degrees and look at the mouth from the front. This will reveal some important variations in the position of the lips and in the shape of the top of the tongue.

First the lips. If you watch yourself in a mirror as you pronounce slowly first *two* and then *eels*, you should notice a marked change from rounded lips to spread lips. Make the same observation as you experiment with other vowels. Each vowel has its own characteristic lip position, just as it has its own characteristic degrees of raising or lowering and fronting or backing of the tongue.

The shape of the top of the tongue is harder to see, but you will probably be able to feel the change as you hold a long *s* sound, then shift to a long *sh* sound, and then switch back and forth between the two *without pausing and without inserting any vowels.* Do the same thing with a long *th* sound (as in path) and an *s* sound. For the *s* sound there is a narrow rill or groove running along the center of the tongue just at the point where you feel the audible turbulence or 'friction.' For *sh* the groove is much wider, and for *th* the top of the tongue is flat. Incidentally, it is the flatness of the tongue that is the essential element in producing the *th* sounds of English, or similar sounds that occur in Greek, Arabic or Swahili. Teachers sometimes tell students that to make these sounds they must stick their tongues out between their teeth. This works if and only if the sticking out of the tongue leads to flattening it. But some students can stick their tongues out and still have that rill running down the middle, while most English speakers make the sound without protruding their tongues. And in some cultures it is considered improper to allow one's tongue to be seen.

There are other phonetic features which result from something that happens in the throat. One which is important in many non-European languages is closure of the vocal cords, or glottis. This 'glottal stop' occurs in English mainly as the boundary between the first and last halves of 'hunh uh,' meaning no. In other languages such as Arabic, Hebrew, Tagalog and Turkish, it appears as an ordinary everyday consonant.

Another consonantal feature is conspicuous in Arabic. This is 'pharyngealization' – a tightening of the pharynx, which is the part of the throat just above the vocal cords.

I hope that this chapter has provided enough details so that each reader will find it helpful in her or his own work. Its purpose, however, is clearly not to provide a comprehensive course in phonetics, but only to start your mind to working with this kind of data.

19 Using the basic equipment

19.1 From features to phonemes

In the preceding chapter, I've described for you some of the principal phonetic features used in the languages that you are likely to be teaching or that your students are likely to speak. But what we ordinarily think of as the 'sounds' of a language – its vowels and its consonants – are phonemes, not features. Phonemes, unlike features, can only be described one language at a time, and within any one language they make up a fairly well organized system of contrasting units. A phoneme is commonly described by listing the phonetic features which it displays.

Take the vowel of English *too*, for example. The usual description for it is 'high back rounded'; 'high' and 'back' on account of tongue position, 'rounded' on account of lip position. Actually, in the more widely used varieties of the language, this sound is also glided or diphthongized, moving toward a higher, farther back, more rounded position from start to finish. In some less widely used varieties of English, the position of the tongue is not at the back of the mouth, but closer to the front. But in English the front and back tongue positions don't contrast with each other for high rounded vowels: any one variety of the language uses one or the other but not both.

French has a high back unrounded vowel also, the one spelled with *ou* as in *vous*. Unlike the English sound, this one is relatively pure or undiphthongized. More important, French has a second high rounded vowel – spelled *u* as in *vu* – which has front tongue position and contrasts with the high back rounded one. English speakers, having been taught by experience with their native language that this difference is meaningless, have learned to ignore it. They therefore find one of the French sounds relatively easy to approximate, and the other one more difficult.

In the same mixture of phonetic and phonemic terminologies,

the first sound in English *do* is a 'voiced apicoalveolar stop.' 'Stop' means that the flow of air is completely cut off, 'alveolar' means that the obstruction is at the gum ridge, and 'apico' means that the tip of the tongue does the obstructing. 'Voiced' means that the vocal cords vibrate during or very soon after the obstruction. Spanish has a similar sound which is 'apicodental'; that is to say, the place where the tongue tip does its obstructing is behind the upper teeth, not at the gum ridge. But when this same Spanish phoneme stands between vowels, it becomes a fricative, something like the English *th* sound in lather. English has a contrast between stop and fricative: *ladder* versus *lather*. Spanish speakers do not have this contrast in their own language, and so they tend to pronounce both of these words as lather.

But this book is neither a text in general phonetics nor an encyclopaedia of the phonemic systems of the world's languages. Because English is a language known to all readers of this book, and because it is so widely taught around the world, I will spend the rest of this chapter on some details of this one language. As you begin to get a feeling for the principles involved, however, you may find yourself noticing new things in the other languages with which you work.

19.2   The consonants and vowels of English

The consonants and vowels of British English, in A. C. Gimson's International Phonetic Alphabet are as follows:

VOWELS AND DIPHTHONGS

i:	*as in* see/si:/	ɜ:	*as in* fur/fɜ:(r)/
ɪ	*as in* sit/sɪt/	ə	*as in* ago/əˈgəʊ/
e	*as in* ten/ten/	eɪ	*as in* page/peɪdʒ/
æ	*as in* hat/hæt/	əʊ	*as in* home/həʊm/
ɑ:	*as in* arm/ɑ:m/	aɪ	*as in* five/faɪv/
ɒ	*as in* got/gɒt/	aʊ	*as in* now/naʊ/
ɔ:	*as in* saw/sɔ:/	ɔɪ	*as in* join/dʒɔɪn/
ʊ	*as in* put/pʊt/	ɪə	*as in* near/nɪə(r))/
u:	*as in* too/tu:/	eə	*as in* hair/heə(r)/
ʌ	*as in* cup/kʌp/	ʊə	*as in* pure/pjʊə(r)/

CONSONANTS

p	*as in* pen/pen/	s	*as in* so/səʊ/
b	*as in* bad/bæd/	z	*as in* zoo/zu:/
t	*as in* tea/ti:/	ʃ	*as in* she/ʃi:/
d	*as in* did/dɪd/	ʒ	*as in* vision/'vɪʒn/
k	*as in* cat/kæt/	h	*as in* how/haʊ/
g	*as in* got/gɒt/	m	*as in* man/mæn/
tʃ	*as in* chin/tʃɪn/	n	*as in* no/nəʊ/
dʒ	*as in* June/dʒu:n/	ŋ	*as in* sing/sɪŋ/
f	*as in* fall/fɔ:l/	l	*as in* leg/leg/
v	*as in* voice/vɔɪs/	r	*as in* red/red/
θ	*as in* thin/θɪn/	j	*as in* yes/jes/
ð	*as in* then/ðen/	w	*as in* wet/wet/

This is the transcription I use in this book.

The consonants and vowels of American English, in the modified version of the International Phonetic Alphabet taken from Clifford H. Prator, Jr.'s *Manual of American English Pronunciation* are as follows:

VOWELS AND DIPHTHONGS

a	*as in* far/far/	o	*as in* go/go/
æ	*as in* am/æm/	u	*as in* rule/rul/
e	*as in* late/let/	ʊ	*as in* put/pʊt/
ɛ	*as in* get/gɛt/	ə	*as in* but/bət/
i	*as in* see/si/	aɪ	*as in* I/aɪ/
ɪ	*as in* in/ɪn/	aʊ	*as in* now/naʊ/
ɔ	*as in* for/fɔr/	ɔɪ	*as in* boy/bɔɪ/

CONSONANTS

b	*as in* boat/bot/	s	*as in* send/sɛnd/
d	*as in* dark/dark/	ʃ	*as in* ship/ʃɪp/
f	*as in* far/far/	t	*as in* ten/tɛn/
g	*as in* gold/gold/	θ	*as in* think/θɪŋk/
h	*as in* home/hom/	ð	*as in* that/ðæt/
k	*as in* cold/kold/	v	*as in* very/'vɛrɪ/
l	*as in* let/lɛt/	w	*as in* went/wɛnt/
m	*as in* man/mæn/	y	*as in* you/yu/
n	*as in* next/nɛkst/	z	*as in* zoo/zu/
ŋ	*as in* ring/rɪŋ/	ʒ	*as in* pleasure/'plɛʒər/
p	*as in* part/part/	tʃ	*as in* children/'tʃɪldrən/
r	*as in* rest/rɛst/	dʒ	*as in* jury/'dʒurɪ/

19.3   Music and meter in English

There's more to pronouncing any language than just stringing together a series of segments made of vowels and consonants. There's also the rise and fall of the voice (the musical 'pitch'), the differing degrees of loudness (stress), the duration of syllables in time ('length') and the overall rhythm of sentences. In speaking any language, if you get any of these 'suprasegmental' features wrong you will have more or less of a 'foreign accent.' Some of these features can also be 'phonemic' (17.2), which is to say that if you get one of them wrong you may find yourself saying something that you didn't mean. Thus in a well known example from Chinese, the single syllable *ma* with four different pitch patterns is four separate words with entirely different meanings. The tone is just as much a part of a Chinese word as the vowel and the consonant are. People who are not accustomed to tone languages often find this example highly exotic and even incredible.

Pitch in English

Languages differ widely from one another in the uses to which they put the 'suprasegmental' features of pitch, stress, length and rhythm. English doesn't use pitch to distinguish between one word and another the way Chinese uses its tones, but it does use patterns consisting of one or more pitches in order to show how one sentence or sentence fragment fits into larger units of speech. So with one pitch pattern the words 'it's raining' will be understood as a simple statement of fact; with a second pitch pattern it comes out as an exclamation of surprise or dismay; with a third it's a question that calls for an answer of yes or no; with a fourth it is followed immediately by something additional, such as 'harder than before' or 'cats and dogs.'

These pitch patterns have always been the subject of a certain amount of misunderstanding. Perhaps the reason is that there are relatively few of them by comparison with the number of words in any language, and that we had pretty much learned all of them before we were old enough to read or write or even talk very much. So they are much deeper parts of us than our vocabulary is – deep enough that we sometimes assume that they are 'just natural' for everyone, and not arbitrary parts of an arbitrary system: 'Of course the voice rises at the end of a question!'

Well, it's true that the pitch rises at the end of 'Is it raining?' but even within English we can document the arbitrariness of the total pattern of pitches in this sentence. In the United States the pitch of *rain* will be higher than the pitch of *it*, while in Britain it will be lower.

The fact that we aren't accustomed to writing pitch patterns as such contributes to a second misunderstanding about the 'melody' of English questions: the assumption that the pitch rises at the end of *all* questions. In American English this is true only for questions that require an answer of yes or no. For those that begin with an interrogative word, such as 'What time is it?' the voice rises and then falls just as it would in a statement. The same words with rising pitch at the end would mean 'Did you ask me what time it is?'

Most of the pitch patterns of English can be represented for language-teaching purposes in terms of three contrasting levels numbered 1, 2, 3 from low to high. You will sometimes find the same levels shown graphically by means of horizontal lines: ^{2}I ^{3}like ^{1}it or I ⌐like⌐ it.

English also makes use of differences in the direction in which the pitch was drifting when last heard at the end of one of these pitch patterns. One way of symbolizing this information is through the use of arrows pointing upward, downward, or horizontally:

It's⌐ raining? ↑   (a question)
It's⌐ rain⌐ing→but I think it will⌐ stop⌐ soon. ↓

The recording of pitch comes naturally to some people, but others find it elusive. Until you are quite sure of yourself in this matter, it will be safer to stick fairly close to examples that you find in books.

Stress

Pitch, then, tells listeners something about how the English words, phrases and sentences that they are hearing fit in with one another, but it does not by itself make the difference between two otherwise identical-sounding words. Stress in English serves a bit of both of these purposes. According to at least one analysis of English, it may be the only audible difference between words: compare *permit* (the noun) and *permit* (the verb) in which the former has main stress on the first syllable, and the latter has main stress on the second. More often a difference in stress is accompanied by a change in vowel quality, but these changes are often of a kind which non-natives fail to hear or produce clearly: e.g. *content* (the noun) and *content* (the adjective). In any case, native speakers of English who are trying to follow what a non-native is saying will be more easily confused by someone who consisTENTly puts the emPHASis on the wrong sylLABle than by someone who conSEEStently treats the two very frequent vowel phonemes of *feet* and *fit* as though they were one.

We saw that pitch in English helps a hearer to keep track of phrases and larger units, and of how they relate to one another. English uses stress – relative loudness – for a similar purpose *within* phrases. There's some disagreement among linguists about the number of contrasting degrees of stress that should be recognized in English. From a strictly auditory point of view, however, and ignoring the niceties of some very astute linguistic analyses, there are apparently three degrees of stress within single words. There are several competing notations for writing them. In one of these systems, which is enjoying increasing popularity, main or primary stress is marked′, secondary stress is marked , and unstressed syllables are left unmarked: ′ con,tract (the noun), con′tract (the verb), con′tractual, ,recre′ate (to create again), recre′ation. A fourth level of stress can show itself when two or more words are combined in a phrase: the ′green,house (where greenhouse is a single word), the ′Greene ′house (with the phrase stress on Greene), the ′green ′house (with the phrase stress on house).

Vowel reduction

The number of vowels and diphthongs which can contrast with one another in the stressed syllables of English is quite large: beat, bit, bait, bet, bat, but, boat and many others. In unstressed syllables this number is much smaller. Thus the first vowels of ahead, effect, pituitary and obtuse will sound the same in the speech of many people, in spite of the differences in spelling. This same limitation on the number of contrasts available in unstressed syllables applies not only to the unstressed syllables within a word, but also to the unstressed words within a phrase. Thus the word *to* when pronounced by itself is the only word in its phrase, and so it receives full stress. Under these circumstances, it has the same vowel as *do*. But in the phrase *to do*, the word that carries the stress is *do*. The word *to* is unstressed, and so its original vowel sound is no longer available to it. Instead, its vowel is now like the first vowel in *ahead*. The most usual symbol for this 'reduced' vowel in English is called 'schwa,' and is written / ə /. This is what is meant by 'vowel reduction in unstressed syllables.' Vowel reduction is a very important feature of spoken English. Students who fail to observe it – who in effect 'over-pronounce' their vowels – make themselves harder to understand, not easier.

Length of syllables

The actual duration of an English syllable measured in hundredths of a second depends partly on the segmental phonemes – the vowels and consonants – that are in it. That, however, is a matter which we can leave to the instrumental phoneticians. Of more practical importance to us as teachers is the fact that, other things being equal, a syllable that is louder (has more stress) also lasts longer: I know *you*; you *know*. This is not true in all languages, even in those that make use of contrasting degrees of stress. In Spanish, for example, *canto* (I sing – stress on first syllable), *cantó* (he/she sang), the length of the syllables stays relatively constant regardless of the position of the stress.

Rhythm

This relationship between stress and length gives to English a characteristic rhythm, in which the time between two heavily stressed syllables tends to be fairly constant no matter how many unstressed syllables stand between them. The best-known example is:

> The d o c tor's   a   s u r geon.
> The d o c tor's   not   a   s u r geon.
> The d o c tor's   not a   good   s u r geon.
> The d o c tor's not a very good s u r geon.

By contrast, the rhythm of a language like Spanish, French or Turkish sounds to an English speaker somewhat staccato and mechanical.

19.4   Some widespread difficulties in pronouncing English

We've already seen (p. 172) that the precise details of pronunciation may vary from language to language even when there is no real danger of misunderstanding. There are several contrasts in English which are absent from many other languages of the

Beyond the classroom

world, and which may therefore cause trouble for students from many parts of the world. The most important of these contrasts are:

1. Between relatively unvarying and relatively diphthongized vowels:

/ɪ/versus/iː/	bit versus beat
/e/versus/eɪ/	bet versus bait
/ʊ/versus/uː/	pull versus pool
/ɔː/versus/əʊ/	caught versus coat

2. Between /æ/ and other vowels:

/æ/versus ɑː/	fad versus father
/æ/versus/e/	bat versus bet

3. Between /ʌ/ and other vowels:

/ʌ/versus/ɒ/or/a/	nut versus not
/ʌ/versus/ɑː/	dunce versus dance (British English)

4. Between /ɜː/ and other vowels:

/ɜː/versus/ɔː/	first versus forced
/ɜː/versus/ɑː/	fur versus far
/ɜː/versus/ɪə/	fir versus fear

5. Between /s/ and /ʃ/ — see versus she
6. Between /tʃ/ and /ʃ/ — chose versus shows
7. Between /r/ and /l/ — road versus load
8. Between /θ/ and /s/ — path versus pass
   or /θ/ and /t/ — path versus pat
   and between /ð/ and /z/ — bathe versus bays
   or /ð/ and /d/ — those versus doze
9. Between /v/ and /w/ — vine versus wine

Some common difficulties arise not from the sound itself, but from having to put a familiar sound into an unaccustomed place.

Many languages contrast *p* and *b* at the beginning and in the middle of words, but at the end of words they have only the voiceless *p*. The same goes for other pairs of consonants: *t* and *d*, *k* and *g*, *f* and *v*, *s* and *z*.

Clusters of two or more familiar consonants may cause trouble, though just which clusters will vary widely according to language background. A few examples are: state versus estate, lobs versus lobbies, object versus (incorrect) *objiect.

182

19.5   On 'foreign accents'

During most of this chapter, we've been looking at 'phonemic' differences in sound – differences which can carry the kind of meaning that you find in a dictionary. Before we leave the subject of pronunciation, let's turn very briefly to the use of phonemic or phonetic (chapter 17) differences in order to convey two other kinds of meaning. You won't ordinarily spend much time in teaching these aspects of the language, at least not overtly. Nevertheless you should understand them well enough so that you won't confound them with each other or with the distinctions that carry dictionary meaning. This is a point which I made in chapter 6, but which is worth further development here.

First, native speakers of a language – *in*voluntarily and sometimes voluntarily – use differences of sound in order to show where they are from or to indicate the social group with which they wish to be identified. Second, overlapping with the first but not identified with it, they use their voices in order to show what they are like personally, or how they feel. Sometimes they do this by choosing between phonemes: in English the word *either* may have the vowel of *buy* or the vowel of *bee*. Other dialect differences are nonphonemic: the phoneme /t/ is usually formed at the gum ridge, but many people in and around New York City make the /t/ sound by placing the tip of the tongue on the upper teeth. Some sounds such as the diphthong of *buy* have so many variant pronunciations that you listen for them when you are trying to guess where a person is from.

The important fact for us as language teachers, however, is not the existence of dialect variations among native speakers. It is rather the symbolic value which those variations carry in expressing a person's identity and loyalties, *whether or not that person is speaking the native language or a foreign one. Dialects* within a language *are made up of choices* between phonemes and between phonetic realizations of phonemes. A 'foreign accent' is made up of non-native choices between phonemes, and non-native phonetic realizations of right phonemes. An accent, whether native or foreign, is at one and the same time a conformity and a nonconformity – an assertion or a surrender of the self-image. Sometimes consciously and sometimes unconsciously, people hold onto wrong and non-native choices because they don't feel ready to be drawn into the unfamiliar and alien world which a new language represents to them. For this reason, there is a limit to what we can do with the sorts of pronunciation practice described in chapter 6. After a certain point we can only remain patient, inviting the other person to sound more like us, but inviting without insistence and without intolerance.

20 Beneath grammar

20.1 Introduction

As language teachers we perform many functions. One of these functions sets us apart in the public mind from other professions more than any other: we are the custodians of something called 'grammar.' It is we who at dinner parties are called upon to settle disputes about whether 'playing' is a participle, a gerund, or something else, and it is we in front of whom parents are most acutely embarrassed when their offspring say 'I seen 'em when they done it.'

This public expectation is based on reality, even though it exaggerates and distorts the place of grammatical knowledge in our work. Materials and techniques are important, keeping students secure and clearly guided is essential, 'communicative' and 'personal' competence (chapter 2) are desirable goals, and we may be right in promoting more 'acquisition' alongside academic 'learning' (chapter 3). Nevertheless, if you are vague in your own mind about the mechanics of sentence structure in the language you are teaching, you will be at a disadvantage. You may still be able to make a lot of good things happen, but you won't be fully able to keep track of what is going on.

20.2 Grammar and the language we are teaching

There are three senses in which we might say that we have some idea about grammar. First, we may be able to apply to our language, in some precise and consistent way, such terms as noun, nominal, substantive, substantival, adverb, aspect, right-branching tree, and so on. This is *theoretical knowledge*, which is expressed in a special language-about-language – a metalanguage. Then there is the ability to see what is in front of one's nose – to focus on form without distraction from meaning or from previous expectations or from anyone else's explanation. This is not so much knowledge as basic *awareness*. Third is accumulation of the observations that we can make when we apply this kind of awareness to the countless facts of a single language, regardless of the metalanguage which we use to state our observations. This is *practical teaching knowledge* of the grammar of that language.

Of these three, the second is clearly the most fundamental. Without it the third is impossible, and the first is only a blind manipulation of formulae. Since this is a book about fundamentals, I shall, in this chapter, show you a few tricks for sharpening your grammatical awareness, but I won't deal with any of the usual metalanguages, and I won't list details about the workings of English or any other language. To try to do either would in any case require too many pages. Most of the examples will be taken from English because that is the only language known to all readers of this book.

Down through the ages, we language teachers must have spent many person-centuries in the activity known as 'discussing grammar.' Our typical answer to a student's question about a point of grammar is (1) long, (2) centered on discussion of 'meanings' and 'logic,' and (3) full of interesting but irrelevant speculation. It therefore does little to fulfill the purpose behind the student's question.

And what *was* the purpose behind the question? As a matter of fact, the student's conscious aim may have been to get just the sort of reply that we so often give: 'I said, "She's working there now" because it's action that's going on in the present. Yes, "She works there now" is also correct, but that is action which is regularly or generally true, and so it requires the simple present tense.' Yet the student's real purpose in asking questions is a part of her total goal in all of her language study: to build the inner resources which will lead her to speak and understand closer to the way natives do. So when she asks what 'part of speech' a word is, she is really asking you to guide her in where to use it; when she asks 'why' a certain construction has unusual word order, she is in effect asking under what circumstances she should use that order. The kind of explanation that I quoted at the beginning of this paragraph is not really very helpful in answering these questions.

The most helpful comments and explanations about grammar are (1) short, (2) may mention meaning, but focus on the audible and visible *forms* of language, and (3) refrain from appeals to history or to the intuitions that a native speaker has. These intuitions will be a by-product of successful exposure to the language, but we can hardly count on them as a means *toward* success. How can you and I, trained as most of us are in an older tradition, learn to make this more useful kind of explanation? The answer begins, as I said earlier in this chapter, with our own basic awareness of the data which lie beneath the rules and explanations.

First, let's be clear about what we *don't* mean by a question of grammar. The choice 'he doesn't' and 'he don't,' for example, is not really a matter of 'grammar' as I am using the word here; it is primarily a question of 'usage.' Quite clearly, the form which we should teach students to produce will almost always turn out to be 'he doesn't,' even though we will hear the other form from many natives. The acceptability of 'The reason is because . . .' is also a question of usage, not of grammar, though I for one find it hard to imagine when I would be willing to teach it to students of English. 'Usage,' then, is concerned with deciding, on the basis of social criteria, which of two competing forms is more prestigious or more widely acceptable.

'Grammar,' as I am using that term here, is a way of telling, as accurately and clearly as possible, just how a particular language arranges its smaller forms – its word stems, prefixes, suffixes, intonations and the like – within its larger constructions such as words, clauses and sentences. A grammatical statement also gives information about the meanings of the constructions which it describes.

The science of making statements about how languages work – and about how language in general works – has been in ferment for many years. Many of the writings in this field will be well worth your study. What I have to say in this chapter is not intended as a substitute for such study, but only to encourage you to take *your own look at some of the data* which the scientists are summarizing in those statements.

Units and hierarchies

'Wait 'til I get to a good stopping place.' No matter what we're doing – painting the porch swing, reading a book, making a dress – we somehow know that certain points are more suitable for stopping than others are. These stopping places help to define the boundaries of the units into which, consciously or unconsciously, we divide our lives and everything we do.

These units may be of almost any size. The larger ones are made up of smaller ones, which in turn are composed of still smaller ones. There is a lower limit beyond which we don't ordinarily go, but each slat in the porch swing is certainly one such unit; the whole seat is a higher-level unit comparable to the whole back; the first coat of paint is a larger unit still. You may find it interesting to pick out units of various sizes in an athletic contest or an academic course or the making of a garden.

Completeness

'And when I found the door was shut, I tried to turn the handle, but . . .' These final words of Humpty-Dumpty to Alice left her thoroughly dissatisfied, for she felt that he really should have gone on and said something further. Psychologists might say that for her the utterance lacked 'closure.' Humpty-Dumpty had stopped, all right; there was no disputing that. But he had stopped at a place where Alice, *on the basis of her past experience with English, had not expected* him to stop. Some strings of words, when spoken with an appropriate intonation contour, have the property of creating a feeling of closure. It is to such strings of words that grammarians apply the label 'sentence.'

Notice that this definition of 'sentence' is not quite like the one that many of us learned in school: 'A sentence is a word or a group of words which expresses a complete thought.' The string of words 'she saw it then' leaves us with that feeling of closure – of being suited for the intonation that normally accompanies such strings – and so we call it a 'sentence.' Its thought is conspicuously incomplete, however, for if we hear the sentence by itself we do not know who she is, or what she saw, or when. On the other hand, the string 'he said he swallowed it' is one sentence and not two or one and a half, even though the last three words by themselves could be a sentence and therefore (by the old definition) 'express a complete thought.'

'Adding up'

*The my father is old.
*Is very old?

I have punctuated these two strings of words as though they were sentences, and their meaning is perfectly clear. Nevertheless, neither of them quite adds up to what speakers of English treat as a 'sentence.' The first contains one word too many, and the second has one word too few. They are, however, word-for-word translations of: *O meu pai é velho. É muito velho?* each of which adds up to a perfectly ordinary sentence in Portuguese.

Customarily when we write a string of words which we want people to interpret as 'adding up' to a single sentence, we begin the first word with a capital letter and place after the last word one of the three marks (.!?). In speaking, we use one of a comparatively small number of intonation contours with such a string.

Working in the opposite direction, if we see a string of words beginning with a capital letter and ending with one of those three punctuation marks, or if we hear a string of words pronounced with one of those same intonation contours, we try to interpret it as 'adding up' to a sentence. The word light, for example, is sometimes 'used as an adjective'; it is then comparable to dark, heavy and other words that we call adjectives. At other times it is 'used as a verb'; then it is comparable to bring and extinguish. Now, if we see the string of words 'Light the lamp.' written in that way, or if we hear those words spoken with an intonation contour that usually goes with sentences, we will try to interpret it as 'adding up.' So if we know that 'bring the lamp' and 'extinguish the lamp' add up, but that 'dark the lamp' and 'heavy the lamp' do not, then we will tend to interpret light in its verbal sense rather than in its adjectival sense. In fact, any other interpretation would not occur to us at all except when we are talking about grammar.

The string '. . . paint around the . . .' is incomplete, and paint could be either a noun or a verb. If you put these words into a complete sentence, you will see how your knowledge of other, parallel sentences, and of the words which could be used in place of paint, are what determine your decision to label it as one part of speech or the other.

The activity that we engage in in order to tell whether light is a noun, verb or adjective is perhaps another example of the recalling and comparison of memories for images, items and patterns about which we talked in chapters 4 and 5.

'Adding up' and 'making sense'

The Portuguese examples at which we have just looked show that a string of words may be intelligible without 'adding up' to a sentence, and that the rules for 'adding up' vary from language to language more than the requirements for making sense do. That of course is why we are able to understand foreigners even when their use of our language contains many errors, and why we are able to correct the errors of our students.

A string of words may also 'add up' unmistakably to a correct sentence without being entirely intelligible: 'The isosceles intonation warbled warmly.' You may be able to provide additional examples of the mutual independence of 'adding up' and 'making sense,' either from English or from other languages that you know.

Grammatical similarity

> attend the conference
> before the conference
> leave the conference

Anyone who uses English will feel that the first and third of these three strings of words are grammatically more like each other than either is like the second. You may already have glanced at them and said, 'Of course! The first and third can be complete imperative sentences, while the second can't!' or 'Of course! Attend and leave are verbs, but before is a preposition!' Each of these formulations is correct enough, of course. The whole point that I am trying to make in this section, however, is exactly that we must distinguish such formulations from the primitive intuitions which lie beneath them. A speaker's ability to say that two strings of words are alike or different in their structure is independent of her ability to label them with grammatical terminology.

'Surroundings'

All right, the strings of words 'attend the conference' and 'leave the conference' are alike in some way or ways which set them apart from the string 'before the conference.' This is an intuition which is shared by everyone who has any control of the language. Now what kind of evidence does memory supply which is consistent with this intuition and may be the source of it? One kind of evidence has to do with the surroundings in which each of these strings may be used. (In the old days before widespread public concern over ecology, the surroundings in which a word or string of words was found was often called its 'environment.')

In this sense, 'attend the conference' and 'leave the conference' can be used in surroundings where 'before the conference' cannot. So for example, 'we must attend the conference' and 'we must leave the conference' add up to complete sentences, but '*we must before the conference' does not. On the other hand, 'they came before the conference' adds up but '*they came attend the conference' does not. It too has its own characteristic set of surroundings in which we can use it.

The preceding paragraph is one simple example of putting our finger on some of the primitive linguistic facts which lie behind the intuitions which in turn lie behind the formulations that we find in the grammatical analyses of theorists. Your goal for your students is only that they develop the intuitions as part of their 'competence' (chapter 2). Reading the formulations and thinking about them may be of help toward this goal, at least for some people, but I think it is more generally useful to lead one's students through some of the more pertinent of these primitive facts. That is indeed the whole point of chapters 8–10 of this book.

This section will mean more to you if you list a few more surroundings in which 'attend/leave the conference' can be used but 'before the conference' cannot, and vice versa.

Degrees of grammatical similarity

The above examples of word strings containing *conference* may have given the impression that intuitively-recognized grammatical similarity is an all-or-none matter. This is not the case, as the following examples will show you if your answers agree with the overwhelming majority of native and non-native speakers with whom I've tested them. According to your intuition, is (a) or (b) grammatically more like the model?

we work hard:	(a) to work hard	(b) they work hard
he reads fast:	(a) she reads well	(b) who reads well
a big dinner:	(a) to cook dinner	(b) a fish dinner
a big dinner:	(a) a hot dinner	(b) a fish dinner
red apples:	(a) eat apples	(b) three apples
red apples:	(a) sour apples	(b) three apples
to school:	(a) to understand	(b) to the barn
to school:	(a) to church	(b) to the barn

'Substitution' as a figure of speech

In the preceding section we saw that the question of whether two strings of words have or do not 'have the same grammatical structure' is not always a simple one for even a native speaker to decide. Grammatical similarity is a matter of degree. Nevertheless, if we are ever to sort language out at all, we must sometimes make an analytical leap and use our intuition to pick out a number of word-strings that we at least suspect of being grammatically equivalent to one another. In many cases our intuitions will prove to have been correct, but we must always test them in terms of what people say and don't say in the language we are studying.

In the case of 'attend the conference,' for example, we might suggest the following tentative equivalents:

> leave the conference
> observe the conference
> study the conference
> advertise the conference

When, as in these examples, the word-strings that we are comparing are alike except for the words in some one part of them, we may use a conventional figure of speech and say that leave, observe, study and advertise have been 'substituted for *attend* in the "slot" .... *the conference*.' This figure of speech is harmless as long as we remember what it stands for.

Working back in the opposite direction, we may begin again with 'attend the conference' and 'make substitutions for' *conference*, such as convention, session, meeting, class. Translated into a statement about word-strings, this substitution list implies that we say:

> attend the convention
> attend the session
> attend the meeting
> attend the class

and that we suspect these strings to be grammatically equivalent to 'attend the conference.'

In the same way you might try out various 'substitutes' in the 'slot' occupied by *the* in these examples: a, that, our, every, for instance.

'Lexical combinations'

If we begin with the word-string 'study the conference,' which we have guessed to be equivalent to 'attend the conference,' we may produce two lists of trial substitutes.

In one slot:

.... the conference

attend
leave
advertise

and in the other:

study the ....

convention
book
assignment

This means that we might use in the first slot in this kind of word-string any of the words in our first list (including *study*) together with *conference* in the last slot; and that we might use in the last slot any of the words in our second list (including *conference*) together with *study* in the first slot. It does not, however, say anything about whether we do or don't use grammatically equivalent utterances made up of other pairings of words from the two lists. We would not, for example, be likely to say:

    * attend the book
    * attend the assignment

That is to say that there are certain combinations of words which we can readily use to fill the slots in this kind of word-string:

    attend .... conference
    study .... conference
    leave .... conference
    study .... book
    study .... assignment

for example, and certain other combinations that we would never (or hardly ever) use there. The examples that I have already given are:

    * attend .... book
    * attend .... assignment

In a sentence with three major slots, such as:

    The bird swallowed the worm.
    The ....ed the ....

some likely combinations are:

    child swallow pin
    snake swallow bird
    cat chase bird

and some unlikely ones are:

```
* bird    swallow   cat
* pin     swallow   child
* house   chase     bird
```

Each of the horizontal rows in the above examples is something that we can call a 'lexical combination.' A 'lexical combination,' then, is a set of word stems which fill the slots in some grammatical construction. It's not a standard term, any more than 'add up' or 'surroundings' are standard terms, but I'll be using it often enough in the next few pages to justify abbreviating it to LC. An LC may have two members (attend, conference) or three members (cat, chase, bird) or even more.

'Modification'

In the preceding section, we in a sense sliced our data horizontally and talked about LC's which fit into pairs (or larger numbers) of slots in grammatically equivalent word-strings. Now let's go back for a moment to the section before that one, where we were in the same sense slicing our data vertically into lists. We spoke there of three 'slots,' and a 'list' that was appropriate to fill each one of them. In terms of linear order, the first slot was the one which could be filled by the list leave, watch, study, advertise; the second could be filled by the list the, a, this, that, our, every; the third could be filled by the list convention, session, meeting, conference. But nothing in what we have said up to this point has given us any indication that the three slots are not all of equal and coordinate status. Yet we find our grammatical intuition rebelling against treating all three of these slots alike. What facts, stated in terms of what we say and don't say, correlate with and presumably lie behind this intuition? Here are a few of them.

We say:

```
she is at   the    conference
            a      convention
            this   session
            that   class
            our    meeting
            every

where is the       conference
        etc.       etc.
```

and we say:
>   she will attend regularly
>   leave
>   etc.
> let's not attend
>   leave
>   etc.

but we don't say:
> * she will attend the regularly
> * she will attend our regularly
> * she will attend a regularly
> * she will attend every regularly

We do of course say 'she will attend this regularly,' but what is important here is that the *whole list* which fitted into 'she is at .... conference' and into '........ conference was a success' does not fit into 'she will attend .... regularly.' (This, incidentally, is a part of what we mean when we say that *that* 'can be used as a pronoun,' while *the* cannot.)

Likewise, we don't say:
> * let's not attend the
> * let's not attend a
>   etc.

Generalizing from these and similar data, we can say that the list which includes *the* precedes the list that includes *conference* in many other surroundings just as it did in our original sentence. On the other hand, there are many places where we find the list that includes *attend*, in which the list that includes *the* may not follow directly after it.

In an apt figure for expressing this generalization, we might call the list that includes *the* a 'satellite' which is related to a 'nucleus.' The 'nucleus' of course consists of the list that includes *conference*. In an extension of this metaphor, we may also say that some one member of the first list is a 'satellite' of some one member of the second list: that in 'attend every session,' the word *every* is a 'satellite' of *session*. This is essentially what we mean when we say, in another figure of speech which is more traditional, that *every* 'modifies' *session* in this string of words. (You may find it worthwhile in consolidating your understanding of this section to marshall examples of what we do and don't say so as to support the conclusion that in 'very old men,' *very* is a 'satellite' of *old*, while in 'nine old men' *nine* is a 'satellite' of *men*. A more difficult enterprise of this kind is to show how *not* fits into the word-string 'the idea is not good.'

Things that have meaning but can't stand alone

We all know what the word *word* means, but defining it is not as easy as it sounds. In fact, there have been many definitions, but none has satisfied everyone. Perhaps the easiest is to say that a word is the shortest thing that people normally pause before and after when they speak, or the shortest thing that they normally put spaces before and after when they write. This rather rough and ready definition leaves some of its own terms undefined, and any linguist will quickly think of borderline cases which it does not handle, but for my purposes here, it will be sufficient.

A 'word' in this very everyday sense has a main part, or 'stem,' which carries the principal dictionary meaning of the word: open in openness, or warm in warmth are examples from English. In many languages including English, the stem is sometimes used as a word by itself.

But in many languages including English, a word often contains other elements in addition to its stem: *-ness* and *-th* in the above examples, but also *-ing* in singing, *-ed* in seated, *un-* in untrue. These other elements don't have such clear dictionary meanings as the stems have; their meanings are more likely to be grammatical and abstract. When these grammatical elements can't stand as separate words, we can think of them as somehow 'tied' or 'bound' to the stems of the words in which we find them. Usually the 'bound forms' of a language make their presence known in the shape of suffixes or prefixes, but sometimes they come out as other changes in the sound or spelling of a word: the past tense part of sang means the same as the past tense part of danced, but its physical form is different.

Incidentally, a bound form of one language may be matched by a separate word in another: approximately the same meaning of definiteness that in English we convey by the word *the* is expressed in Armenian by a suffix, and in Arabic or Hebrew by a prefix.

Language teachers have traditionally and necessarily paid special attention to the bound forms of their languages. Bound forms tend to be relatively limited in number: some languages have almost none, others may have a few dozen. Bound forms also tend to be relatively steady in their habits: each knows its own place relative to the stem and to other prefixes and suffixes. For these two reasons, it is easy to draw up rules and diagrams that summarize how bound forms are used; this gives us something clear to teach. It is also easy to detect and point out errors in the use of bound forms; a cynic might say that this helps to keep us in business.

What the speakers have picked up about bound forms also serves as an important source of the intuitions that are formulated as grammatical terminologies. The words in one of the lists that we've been talking about are likely to agree with one another in the bound forms they can take, and to differ from the words in another list in that respect. In the example that we've been using, the list attend, leave, observe and study can form a past tense and can take the suffix *-ing* but cannot form a plural. The list conference, session, class, convention can form a plural but not a past tense, and does not accept the suffix *-ing*.

This kind of information, together with the information drawn from knowledge about lists, slots and lexical combinations, gives rise to the 'parts of speech': nouns, verbs, adjectives and all the rest. When students ask questions about what part of speech a word is, they are really (whether they are aware of it or not) asking for help in using the word correctly in the future. They may expect you to come back with some reply such as 'It's a pronoun' or 'an adjective' or 'a pronominal adjective' or 'an adjectival pronoun,' or 'It's a noun functioning as an adjective' or 'a prepositional phrase used as the object of a preposition' or something similar. Such a reply can be helpful and time-saving, but only if you and they share the same underlying intuitions about what these terms stand for in terms of what people do and don't say in the language.

Take for example a question that someone once asked me: 'What part of speech is *then* in the sentence: "The then president refused to call a meeting." Is it an adverb because it answers the question when? Or is it an adjective because it modifies a noun? Or is this an unusual case of an adverb modifying a noun?' This sort of question can be misleading because it assumes that there are eight (or 18 or 48 or 80) categories called 'parts of speech.' Some of the information that the questioner found helpful included the fact that there are a few other time expressions which can also modify nouns. They include *now* and *future*, but not *Sunday, on Sunday,* or *two years ago.* We say 'She was president then' and 'the then president,' 'She was

president two years ago,' but not 'the two years ago president.'
Slots and lists, rather than labels, are the focus here.

'Lexical combinations' in superficially different constructions

In English we can quite normally say:
> the teacher is happy
> the teacher is sad
> the teacher is earnest
> the teacher is short

but we would be much less likely to say:
> the teacher is massive

and it is very hard to imagine a situation when we would want
to say:
> the teacher is hydrogenated

Putting *teacher* into new settings, we do say:
> the happy teacher is here
> he paid the happy teacher a compliment
> she commented on the happiness of the teacher

Into any of these sentences we can readily substitute sad, earnest
or short in the slot occupied by *happy*. We would be unlikely to
use *massive* here, and *hydrogenated* would make as little sense
here as it did in the first example. But if a situation were to arise
in which we did feel moved to say:
> the teacher is massive

we could *just as easily* say:
> the massive teacher is here
> he paid the massive teacher a compliment
> she commented on the massiveness of the teacher

and the same is true for hydrogenated.

My point here is that the *likelihood* of a given pair of words
being used together in a given pair of slots is *to a large degree
independent of the phrase structure* of the sentence in which the
words occur. *It is this fact which makes such 'co-occurrence
restrictions' between words interesting to the grammarian as
well as to the lexicographer.*

'Transforms'

A further example of this point is provided by
> the teacher attended the meeting
> the   (1)   (2) ed the   (3)

which we recognize as a 'complete sentence,' and

the teacher's attending the meeting
the (1) 's (2) ing the (3)
which we call a 'noun phrase.' The two are different constructions, but LC's which satisfy one satisfy the other.

If we present to speakers of English the sentence
the cat is smarter than the dog
they will accept it as perfectly normal. If we suggest the sentence
the cat is smarter than the mountain
it will be rejected, probably with the comment that 'mountains
aren't smart.' We can put the same thing in terms of what people
do and don't say: a sentence of the form
the (1) is (2)er than the (3)
implies the existence of simpler sentences:
the (1) is (2)
the (3) is (2)
In one figure of speech which linguists sometimes use, the two
simpler sentences 'underlie' the longer one; in another figure of
speech, the simpler ones are related to the more complex one
through a process of 'transformation.' A style of grammatical
description which does not take into account this sort of
relationship cannot distinguish between the structure of
Dagwood called Mr Dithers a taxi.
and
Dagwood called Mr Dithers a tyrant.
even though intuitively we feel that they are different. A style of
description which does take this sort of relationship into
account, on the other hand, can assign to each of these sentences
a different transformational history, thereby corroborating and
illuminating intuition. This is why such descriptions can be
useful to teachers and students as well as to theoreticians.

20.3 Conclusion

This is a book of beginnings, written first of all for beginners. It
is, moreover, about learning and teaching languages and not
about language. It is about practice and not about theory. That
is why I have written this chapter as I have. Nevertheless even a
new teacher will benefit indirectly from what linguistic theorists
have done. As you go along you will probably begin to welcome
direct contact with their work.

In recent years we have sometimes talked about language
teaching as one branch of 'applied linguistics.' But it seems to

me that to talk about 'applying' a theory or a body of knowledge can be misleading. It can be misleading because we too easily take it to mean that the theory or the body of knowledge is somehow primary and that our 'applications' are secondary to it. This is like deciding the old conundrum by declaring that it was the chicken (or the egg) which came first. A theory, after all, is nothing but a guess about how a certain body of knowledge hangs together. A body of knowledge, in turn, grows one molecule at a time out of experience – including *our* experiences. When we set out to 'apply' linguistics or psychology or any other scholarly discipline, we do draw light from it. But we also test it and thus cast light back onto it by contributing toward its eventual confirmation or toward its alteration.

What I have said in the preceding paragraph is of course a commonplace, even to the point of being platitudinous. Yet how often at professional meetings it is the theorist who is lionized – and who is given the lion's share of the respect! I am not saying that we do not need theorists or that we should not respect them. I'm only saying that a practitioner also has her or his own kind of primacy. Read the theorists with interest but also with independence, and save some of your respect for yourself!

21 Beyond this book: further reading

21.1 Introduction

There is more to teaching language than you will find between
the covers of this book, or of any other book. In this final
chapter, therefore, I will point you to some of the other sources
that you may find helpful as you get started in our profession. In
1947, when I was beginning to teach English as a second
language, there weren't many books in the field. Now there are
dozens of books just for teachers, not to mention hundreds of
textbooks for teaching the major languages. I must therefore
limit myself to a few of the best ones that happen to have come
to my attention. I'll stick to relatively practical books; as you get
your bearings in the profession, you'll find for yourself the more
theoretical ones that interest you.

Yes, there is more to teaching language than what is in this
book, and there is more to language teaching than teaching
language. Teaching language is only one kind of teaching, and
teaching and learning are only two limited aspects of being
human. I therefore hope, first of all, that you will take time to sit
down and read again whatever philosophical or religious writings you have found most nourishing to you.

21.2 General background

Let me begin with three maxims which for me are at the heart of
Caleb Gattegno's *Silent way*:
> Watch.
> Give only what is needed.
> Wait.

I think that people who read his *The common sense of teaching
foreign languages* (Educational Solutions, 1976) will find the
first chapter of his *Who cares about health?* (Educational
Solutions, 1979) to be an illuminating companion to that book.

A source that has helped me to clarify for myself the nature of learning, and what a teacher should and should not reasonably try to do, is W. Timothy Gallwey's *The inner game of tennis* (Random House, 1974). As its title suggests, this is a book written by a tennis coach for tennis players. It is, however, brief and readable, and its very distance from language teaching may help to put our field into perspective.

A book which bears a similar message but carries it farther is Betty Edwards' *Drawing on the right side of the brain* (Tarcher, 1979). It also has interesting things to say about the differences between the right and left hemispheres of the brain. The book itself is relatively inexpensive, and trying out the author's suggestions is just plain cheap. All it takes is pencil, paper and a little time. Aside from what I have learned from them, I have found the exercises to be great fun.

A readable historical survey is *Twenty-five centuries of language teaching*, by Louis G. Kelly (Newbury House, 1969). One salutary effect of reading this book is that it should keep you from being bowled over by periodic swings of the great methodological pendulum, or from regarding as benighted all those who have not seen the light of the most recent theory, or from mortgaging your home in order to buy the latest piece of pedagogical hardware.

In the first two and last chapters of *Teaching languages: a way and ways* (Newbury House, 1980), I tried to put language teaching into a wider framework, particularly in relation to some ideas I found in writings by Dostoyevsky and the late Ernest Becker. The general theme was that, in a psychological sense, what goes on in a language class is often a matter of life and death. A short story which, for me at least, illuminates this point is 'A clean, well-lighted place,' by Ernest Hemingway.

A book that served to put things into perspective for many of us was Wilga Rivers' *The psychologist and the foreign-language teacher* (University of Chicago Press, 1964). This book is no longer recent, and the controversy to which it was addressed has largely subsided, but its basic points will be of interest generation after generation.

Another source of perspective among the competing methods is *The language teaching controversy*, by Karl Diller (Newbury House, 1978). It is both sensible and well written.

A very helpful summary of issues that are current in the profession as I write this chapter (1981) is H. Douglas Brown's

Principles of language learning and teaching (Prentice-Hall, 1980).

My view of the fundamental importance of the student's security (p. 6) came from writings of the late Charles A. Curran. Of these, the one of most direct interest to language teachers is his *Counseling – learning in second languages* (Apple River Press, 1976).

21.3 Part 1

These have been a few sources of general background. As you continue your professional education, however, much of what you read will be about very specific things that you can do in the classroom, and you will also attend countless demonstrations of 'the latest thing.' As you do so, there's a set of distinctions which can help you to avoid a lot of unnecessary confusion. In 1963, Edward M. Anthony published an article which has since become a classic. It was titled 'Approach, method and technique.' These three words are sometimes used interchangeably, but Anthony assigned them meanings which correspond to quite different levels of abstraction.

As Anthony used the terms, an 'approach' is a set of assumptions about the nature of learning and teaching: that a language is primarily a set of physical habits, perhaps, or that it is the product of a special language acquisition device peculiar to the human species; that students are motivated principally by a desire to get the right answer, or by a desire to enhance their own self-esteem; assumptions in these and other areas.

A 'technique,' in Anthony's sense, is simply something that we do: showing a picture to our students and talking about it with them in a certain way; having the class repeat sentences in chorus, and so forth. A 'method,' then, is a set of techniques which fit well together and which are consistent with some approach or other.

What happens too often is this: A teacher attends a demonstration of something new. That something may be an approach, a method or a technique. (You can't always tell by reading the title of the demonstration, because the people who are doing the demonstrating don't always conform to Anthony's use of these three words.) Even if the labeling is clear, however, there's still a likelihood of confusion. Suppose that the purpose of the demonstration is in fact to introduce an unfamiliar approach. Whatever the approach may be, it cannot be demonstrated without employing one or more techniques. These techniques will – and should – be chosen so as to fit the audience, the demonstration students, and the time and facilities that are available. Ideally, a member of the audience will watch one or more demonstrations, listen to explanations, and form in his own head an understanding of the set of principles – the approach – that stands behind the visible and audible demonstration. Then, when he experiments with it on his own, he will try to apply those same principles, again taking into account the students, the time and facilities available, and so on.

Frequently, however, teachers watch the externals of the demonstration without digging very hard for the principles. Back in their own classrooms, they try to copy the technique as closely as possible. This may lead to poorly understood failure or – almost as unfortunate – to poorly understood success. It also often happens that watching activity without understanding principles leads to bizarrely distorted perceptions of the activity itself. Such distortion has in the past done great mischief.

Teachers also sometimes devise their own 'methods' by pulling together a few techniques that appeal to them. Anthony's three-way distinction reminds us that it will be worth our while to look at our own favorite techniques to see how they fit together, and to notice what assumptions they imply.

The beginning of this chapter was concerned with writings which will help you to understand writings – with general background. The remaining pages contain references which are more specific, many of them tied to points in chapters 1–20. Here, and particularly where I mention books which students use in the classrooms, my listings are very incomplete; inclusion or omission of any one item is to a certain extent fortuitous – some may say capricious. I believe that everything I have mentioned is good, but I have not mentioned – or even seen – everything that is worth looking at.

A few years ago, David Blot and Phyllis Sher published *Getting into it: an unfinished book* (Language Innovations Incorporated, 1978). It consists of a number of vignettes, each telling from the point of view of a different student something of what it's like to use and to study a second language. It was intended for use with students, and you may want to use it with yours. I mention it here, however, for the insights which we teachers can extract from its brief, convincing narratives, each drawn from one or more real people. In this respect it illuminates several of the points that I made in chapter 1.

My own awareness of the importance of unnoticed nonverbal behavior (chapter 1) has come largely from the work of Georgi Lozanov. His major book, *Suggestology and outlines of suggestopedy* (Gordon and Breach, 1978) is highly technical and a bit formidable. I devoted two chapters of *A way and ways* to some of his ideas. Other writers, whose direct knowledge of Suggestopaedia vastly exceeds mine, are: W. Jane Bancroft, especially her article on 'The Lozanov method and its American adaptations' in the *Modern Language Journal*, 1978; Fanny Saféris' *Une révolution dans l'art d'apprendre* (Robert Laffont, 1978); and the *Journal of the Society for Suggestive-Accelerative Learning and Teaching*.

The Stravinsky quotation in chapter 1 is from *Poetics of music in the form of six lessons* (Harvard University Press, 1942). This little book is well worth reading in its own right, though of course it is not about teaching foreign languages.

For an early and influential discussion of 'performance' and various kinds of 'competence' (chapter 2) you may want to read Dell Hymes' 'On communicative competence.' It is conveniently available in *The communicative approach to language teaching*, edited by C. J. Brumfit and K. Johnson (Oxford University Press, 1979). This is an anthology which contains several other excellent articles as well.

A writer who has explored the contrast between 'learning' and 'acquisition' (chapter 3) is Stephen D. Krashen. His many writings on this subject include *Second language acquisition and second language learning* (Pergamon, 1981). Another view of how a language learner's mind works is found in John H. Schumann's *The pidginization process: a model for second language acquisition* (Newbury House, 1978). This topic is discussed by contributors to such journals as *Language Learning, International Review of Applied Linguistics,* and *Applied Psycholinguistics*.

The first three chapters of my *Memory, meaning and method* (Newbury House, 1976) summarize certain research findings on remembering and forgetting.

The use of physical activity (chapter 4) as a continuous and integral part of learning has been a particular concern of James J. Asher. See *Learning another language through actions: the complete teacher's guidebook* (Sky Oak Productions, 1977).

Two recently and extraordinarily well written books on how the mind works with language and with memories are *Psychology and language* by Herbert H. Clark and Eve V. Clark, (Harcourt Brace Jovanovich, 1977) and *Human cognition*, by John D. Bransford (Wadsworth, 1979). These books would be excellent collateral reading for chapters 4 and 5.

A multivolume work in the field is S. P. Corder and J. P. B. Allen's *Edinburgh course in applied linguistics* (Oxford University Press, 1974).

21.4 Part 2

Among the journals which historically have given most space to classroom techniques are *English Language Teaching Journal* and *Foreign Language Annals*. *TESOL Quarterly* and *Modern Language Journal* combine practical and general articles. These and other journals can be excellent companions for you as you explore what is in Part 2 (chapters 6–16).

Two books which I have found to be especially rich sources of techniques of all kinds are Wilga Rivers' *Teaching foreign language skills*, originally published by the University of Chicago Press in 1968, new edition published in 1981; and Wilga Rivers and Mary Temperley's *A practical guide to the teaching of English* (Oxford University Press, 1977). Rivers has published a similar book for the teaching of French, and with other collaborators for the teaching of German and Spanish. Another book which provides clear examples of techniques within a single method is *Teaching English as a second language,* by C. B. Paulston and M. Bruder (Winthrop, 1976).

The experiences out of which I have written this book were with adult students. A book on working with children is *Teaching foreign languages to the very young,* edited by Reinhold Freudenstein (Pergamon, 1979). A standard text on the same subject is Mary Finocchiaro's *Teaching children foreign languages* (McGraw-Hill, 1964).

A textbook that exemplifies the 'Functional–Notional' approach to materials-writing is *Strategies* by Abbs, Ayton and Freebairn (Longman, 1975). It combines lively and realistic fictional matter with opportunities for students to use the same language in talking about real facts. The approach itself is set forth in D. A. Wilkins' *Notional syllabuses* (Oxford University Press, 1976).

Some of the suggestions for oral drilling (chapter 6) are from P. Gurrey's *Teaching English as a foreign language* (Longman, 1955). This is a book that I found helpful in my own days as a beginning teacher.

In her *Jazz chants* (Oxford University Press, 1978), Carolyn Graham demonstrates an appealing and powerful way to use rhythm as a means for making new language a part of people (chapter 6). A book which provides original words which students sing to familiar tunes is Uwe Kind's *Tune into English* (Regents, 1980).

Two classical statements of Audiolingualism and the assumptions behind it (chapters 6–8) were Nelson Brooks' *Language and language learning: theory and practice* (Harcourt Brace Jovanovich, 1960) and William G. Moulton's *Linguistic guide to language learning* (Modern Language Association of America, 1966). Even earlier, and of great influence particularly in the United States, was Charles C. Fries' *Teaching and learning English as a foreign language* (University of Michigan Press, 1945).

For a modern view of reading as an active process (chapter 6), read Frank Smith's *Understanding reading* (Holt, Rinehart and Winston, second edition 1978).

The potential values of selective listening (chapter 6) were first set forth by Eugene Nida in his *Learning a foreign language* (Friendship Press, 1957).

Two books about the subject of chapter 6 are *The teaching of pronunciation*, by Peter MacCarthy (Cambridge University Press, 1978) and *The teaching of pronunciation*, by Brita Haycraft (Longman, 1971).

The practice of standing behind students while giving them new words (chapter 6) is one fragment of the technique most frequently associated with 'Community Language Learning,' a method which developed out of Charles A. Curran's 'Counseling–learning' approach. See the book reference near the beginning of this chapter.

A system built around filmstrips of colored drawings (chapter 7) is the Audiovisual global method of Guberina and Rivenc, originally produced for French under the title *Voix et images de France* (Didier, 1959). It is now available in a number of other languages.

The idea of systematically varying your tone of voice when reading aloud material which you hope students will later reproduce (chapter 7) is a fragment of Suggestopaedic technique. See the earlier reference to the work of Lozanov. The use of contrasting colors for words of different types (p. 78) is borrowed from Community Language Learning, already mentioned in this chapter.

For discussion and examples of relatively lively teaching of material which has traditionally been dull (chapter 8), see in the Brumfit and Johnson anthology, Henry Widdowson's article on 'The teaching of English as communication,' the article by J. P. B. Allen and Henry Widdowson on 'Teaching the communicative use of English,' and the extracts from various teaching materials given at the end of the book. A book-length systematic treatment of this subject is William T. Littlewood's *Communicative language teaching* (Cambridge University Press, 1981).

The fifth use of tape recordings (chapter 11) is taken from *Sounds interesting*, by Alan Maley and Alan Duff (Cambridge University Press, 1975). The seventh is based on one aspect of Suggestopaedia.

As you work with audiovisuals (chapter 11), you may profit from consulting *Visual materials for the language teacher*, by Andrew Wright (Longman, 1976). (A series of books that makes vigorous and varied use of pictures is *Méthode orange* by Reboullet, Malandain and Verdol, a French course for children published by Hachette-Regents in 1978.) Julian Dakin has written on *The language laboratory and language learning* (Longman, 1973).

Having students talk about themselves, their experiences and their values (chapter 12) can be a powerful way of breathing life into what goes on in the classroom. A number of writers have been developing this insight, among them Beverly Wattenmaker and Virginia Wilson in their *A guidebook for teaching English as a second language* (Allyn and Bacon, 1980); Beverly Galyean in her 'Confluent' approach; Gertrude Moskowitz in *Caring and sharing in the foreign language class* (Newbury House, 1978); Fraida Dubin and Elite Oltshain in *Facilitating language learning* (McGraw-Hill, 1977).

Some books for students are written in language which is grammatically correct but which is so earnest and flat that it contributes nothing to the aesthetic motivation of either student or teacher. One book which treats even very simple matters with subtle excellence of style, and which at the same time invites students to explore and express their own thoughts is *Prose and passion*, by Gary Gabriel (Regents, 1981).

The basic principles of games as I have described them in chapter 13 are taken from unpublished papers by John Francis and/or John H. T. Harvey. Another source of ideas is Wright, Betteridge and Buckby's *Games for language learning* (Cambridge University Press, 1979).

I first saw the Word-card game (13.3) used by Keiko Komiya in a Japanese class at one of Curran's Counseling-Learning Institutes.

The Gabelentz quotation at the beginning of chapter 14 is only one gem out of *How to teach a foreign language*, by Otto Jespersen (Allen and Unwin, 1947). First published in 1904, this little book is valuable as much for its spirit as for its techniques. The variants on the Tell and show game in chapter 14 were reported by Larry Cesar in an article in *TESOL Newsletter*.

A book that provides topics and material for one side of a series of debates is *For and against*, by L. G. Alexander (Longman, 1969). A recent book on getting people to talk is *Discussions that work*, by Penny Ur (Cambridge University Press, 1981), and a book that contains simulation practice (14.6) is *Eight simulations*, by Leo Jones (Cambridge University Press, 1982).

A systematic treatment of materials adaptation, with a wide variety of examples, is *Adaptation in language teaching*, by Harold S. Madsen and J. Donald Bowen (Newbury House, 1978). This book goes far beyond what I have been able to say in chapter 16.

Drama techniques in language learning, by Alan Maley and Alan Duff (Cambridge University Press, 1978) is the source of the little conversation on page 164. More important, its opening chapter is a brief and exquisitely written sketch of some of the areas that linguists study. A quite different but equally stimulating use of drama in the language classroom is described by Richard Via in *English in three acts* (University Press of Hawaii, 1976).

21.5 Part 3

An anthology with a large number of extremely short readings from the literature on language teaching is *English teaching perspectives*, edited by Donn Byrne (Longman, 1980).

As students move from zero knowledge toward mastery, their

language passes through a number of intermediate stages. The mistakes that they make can help us to understand this process and keep track of it in our own classes. A book on this subject is *Error analysis*, edited by Jack Richards (Longman, 1974).

To some extent at least, the difficulties that students meet arise out of the differences between their native language and the language they are learning. Carl James' *Contrastive analysis* (Longman, 1980) examines this facet of our work. You may want to read this alongside or after chapters 18–20.

A much fuller set of facial diagrams for the sounds of English (chapter 18) is found in my *Workbook in language teaching* (Abingdon Press, 1963), which is also the source for the treatment of grammar in chapter 20 of this book.

21.6 Conclusion

It has been truly said that of the making of many books there is no end. In this closing chapter I have set you in the midst of a whole throng of books. Now we have come to the end of yet another book, and I must leave you alone just as you were alone before you began to read my words — just as you have really been alone in reading. Your work is in your hands. My hope is that you will see, perhaps a little more fully than before, how the choices that you make fit into what goes on inside and among the people in your classroom.

Index

213